INTO GOD'S PRESENCE

Other Publications by Liz Babbs

A Quiet Place, CD. Suffolk: Kevin Mayhew, 2004.

Out of the Depths, book and CD.
    Suffolk: Kevin Mayhew, 2004.

Can God Help M.E?
    Milton Keynes: Authentic Media, 2005.

The Celtic Heart, book and CD. Oxford: Lion, 2003.

The Thing about Calories. Oxford: Lion, 2003.

The Thing about the Office. Oxford: Lion, 2003.

The Thing about Stress. Oxford: Lion, 2002.

For more details visit Liz Babbs' web page
    www.lizbabbs.com or email *liz@lizbabbs.com*.

INTO GOD'S PRESENCE

Listening to God through
Prayer and Meditation

LIZ BABBS

GRAND RAPIDS, MICHIGAN 49530 USA

ZONDERVAN™

Into God's Presence
Copyright © 2005 by Elizabeth Babbs

Requests for information should be addressed to:

Zondervan, *Grand Rapids, Michigan 49530*

Elizabeth Babbs hereby asserts her moral right to be identified as the author of this work.

Library of Congress Cataloging-in-Publication Data

Babbs, Elizabeth.
    Into God's presence : listening to God through prayer and meditation / Liz Babbs. – 1st ed.
        p. cm.
    Includes bibliographical references.
    ISBN 0-310-25240-7 (hardcover: alk. paper)
    1. Contemplation. 2. Prayer – Christianity. 3. Bible – Meditations. I. Title.
    BV5091.C7B28 2005
    248.3'4—dc22

2004018010

This edition printed on acid-free paper.

Every effort has been made to trace the acknowledged copyright holders of all the quotations in this book. We apologize for any errors or omissions that may remain and would ask those concerned to contact the publishers, who will ensure that full acknowledgement is made in the future.

The website addresses recommended throughout this book are offered as a resource to you. These websites are not intended in any way to be or imply an endorsement on the part of Zondervan, nor do we vouch for their content for the life of this book.

Interior design by Beth Shagene

Printed in the United States of America

---

05 06 07 08 09 10 11 /❖ DCI/ 10 9 8 7 6 5 4 3 2 1

Contents

Dedicated to all my friends,
who have so faithfully prayed and supported me
while I've been writing this book.

Foreword by Rev Dr Rob Frost

In a spiritual age, Christians are rediscovering the ancient disciplines of Christian mysticism. Liz Babbs' book gives a friendly and approachable introduction to Christian meditation, and my hope is that it will stimulate many to venture into an enriching and rewarding new journey with Jesus Christ.

Meditation is at the heart of the church's expertise. The more I study it, the more I come to the conclusion that we've let the world steal this treasure away from us. The pathetic pile of meditation cards sold in New Age meditation kits seem a poor alternative to the thousands of years of experience which the church has in its treasure store!

The writings of the great mystics demonstrate that Christian meditation begins with an overwhelming sense of eternity and timelessness. In Christian mysticism we begin by being 'engulfed by the divine'. We need to begin with what Theodore Roosevelt, one of the most powerful men in the world, used to call 'cutting down to size'. William Beebe described it in these words:

> Theodore Roosevelt and I used to play a little game together. After an evening of talk, we would go out on the lawn and search the skies until we found the faint spot of light-mist

beyond the lower left-hand corner of the Great Square of Pegasus. Then one or the other of us would recite: 'That is the spiral galaxy in Andromeda. It is as large as our Milky Way. It is one of a hundred million galaxies. It consists of one hundred million suns, each larger than our sun.' Then Roosevelt would grin at me and say: 'Now I think we are small enough! Let's go to bed. [from Donald E. Miller, *Reinventing American Protestantism*. Univ. of Calif., 1997.]

In an increasingly spiritual age in which words seem to clutter our consciousness rather than liberate it, I want to be 'cut down to size'. I want to enter into the experience of the Psalmist, who, in Psalm 46:10 wrote: 'Be still, and know that I am God.'

The evangelists were the peacemakers of eighteenth-century Christianity, the missionaries led the way in the nine-teenth century, and the martyrs have been at the forefront of Christian witness in the twentieth century. I believe that it is the Christian mystics who will be the ones with much to say to a postmodern society. They will model how to live in the stillness of the presence of God and will play a significant role in shaping the society of the twenty-first century.

The current disillusionment with consumerism, material-ism and the mass production of our age has driven many to seek a richer 'interconnectedness' and to hunger for a new harmony with nature and the changing seasons. Essentially, this is a hunger for God, and I share it with them.

In a world of growing pressure and pain, I need to dis-cover a form of Christian spirituality which does not separate me from the world . . . but which enables me to find the still-ness of God's presence in the thick of the action! I want to nurture that relationship with Christ which is at the heart of true Christian experience. I want to give it time and learn how to 'practise the presence of Christ'.

I take seriously the need for a focused life of prayer. My life must model that prayer leads me to a richer quality of life, a more healthy perspective, and a holistic perception of myself. I want to be a Spiritually Alive Christian, to leave behind my earthly thoughts and reasoning, my daily preoccupation with the self . . . and discover the greatness, the reality, the glory and the Presence of God.

The Psalmists were driven by this mystical passion for the re-awakening of God consciousness. Their poetry gives evidence again and again of a sense of abiding communion, and of the reality of a Divine Presence not confined to time or place. They are linked to God in an enduring unity. So, today I will find a quiet location. Wear casual clothing. Put on some helpful music. Light a candle. Pick up my Bible and read:

> Yet I am always with you;
> You hold me by my right hand.
> You guide me with your counsel,
> And afterwards you will take me into glory.
> Whom have I in heaven but you?
> And earth has nothing I desire besides you.
> Psalm 73:23–25

I will let the words roll around my experience and begin to meditate on the closeness and love of God. I will practise the presence of God and allow him to take me on a journey with a destination, a journey into his healing, restoring love. A journey into a new Christian experience.

I believe that through meditation God wants to give us new perspectives on old situations—his perspectives. I believe as we give ourselves to him in worship and the word and in relationship and in prayer, we begin to gain his perspective and find beauty and grace. Our situation may not change—but we will. And that enables us to rejoice in hope, to find hope.

Introduction

It's hard enough to pray anyway. Do I really need another book to make me feel guilty about my prayer life?

Don't worry, I'm not about to unloose a series of spiritual body blows that begin with 'You Must . . .' or 'You Ought . . .' I know what it's like to bash yourself on the head with a daily dose of self-condemnation.

Most of us find prayer and Bible study difficult, and we dread being asked about our prayer life. It's like being back at school and not having done your homework – you'll make up any excuse so that you don't appear to be a bad Christian.

I think we'd all do each other a favour by admitting how hard we find it to pray and how much we struggle to find the time or even the inclination. God wants us to be real with him, so perhaps we need to be more real with each other too. Even Jesus' disciples asked him how to pray! Jesus responds to us today as he did to his disciples – with an invitation to come and learn about prayer from him, the One whose 'yoke is easy', and he reassures us with these words:

> Are you tired? Worn out? Burned out on religion? Come to me. Get away with me and you'll recover your life. I'll show you how to take a real rest. Walk with me and work with

me – watch how I do it. Learn the unforced rhythms of grace. I won't lay anything heavy or ill-fitting on you. Keep company with me and you'll learn how to live freely and lightly. (Matthew 11:28–30 MSG)

Still, living 'freely and lightly' is not easy to do. One time, for instance, I was alarmed to read that I had been billed in the advertising literature of a particular Christian conference as an 'expert in relaxation and meditation'. It was enough to send me into an immediate stress reaction. I'm still a 'work in progress', wrestling with my achievement-orientated personality.

'Expert in meditation' I am not – but experienced in meditation I am. Having chatted with monks, nuns and bishops on the subject, I am convinced that there is no such thing as an expert anyway. Our prayer life is a journey, with its inevitable ups and downs. The reassuring fact is that nobody has arrived – it's an ongoing journey heavenward. All relationships fluctuate and take time to build and maintain, but I'm sure that God loves it even if we can only spend a minute with him. Wouldn't you love to spend a minute with your closest friend?

Initially, I had no idea how to meditate. The books I found on the subject were complicated, inaccessible and seemed to be written by spiritual athletes. I wanted a simple 'how to' guide without any jargon, an ABC approach to the subject – a what, when, where, how, why with plenty of examples that fitted my lifestyle, not the lifestyle of a monk or nun.

I hope you find this book goes some way towards addressing that need.

CHAPTER 1

What Is Meditation?

∞

∞ The Spiritual Supermarket

Spirituality is a popular word these days. In fact, an awareness of all things spiritual has multiplied in the past decade and created something of a spiritual supermarket. Even the word *spiritual* has been taken over by our consumerist culture and is seen as simply another way to get more out of life.

Not surprisingly, meditation techniques are becoming increasingly popular. In this age of self-help and self-enlightenment, many see it simply as a means to de-stress and achieve a sense of peace and well-being.

For the Christian, however, spirituality is not about getting more; it is, rather, essentially about relationship – a relationship focused on God, which embraces every aspect of one's being. Centred on the teachings of Jesus, this relationship involves Bible study, prayer and contemplation.

When some people hear the word *meditation*, an automatic word association takes place; for them, *meditation* equals *transcendental meditation* (TM). This is understandable because back in the 1960s, the Beatles popularised this form of meditation, and so all meditation became synonymous with TM.

Many people don't even realise that TM has a religious origin – in Hinduism.

Unfortunately, many Christians seem to be unaware of their own rich tradition in meditation – a tradition that originates in the Bible! The church has done little to encourage us to explore our roots in Christian meditation, a fact that has not only contributed to our current spiritual poverty but has also meant that we are not being heard as Christians in today's spiritual marketplace. It's not surprising then that many describe meditation and contemplative prayer as 'the best kept secret in the church'.

∞ Christian Meditation

I first stumbled across Christian meditation when I was ill with ME (which stands for *myalgic encephalomyelitis*, also called 'chronic fatigue syndrome') some fourteen years ago. Much was being said at the time about the benefits of transcendental meditation for those with chronic fatigue, but I was unhappy about the non-Christian principles underlying this form of meditation.

Some months later, however, another Christian ME sufferer gave me a little booklet called *Meditation – Why and How* by Rev. Leonard C. Wilson. I was amazed because I had no idea that there was a Christian form of meditation or that it was referred to as 'contemplative prayer'. The booklet gives an excellent description of meditation:

> Meditation is a mental and spiritual activity between an individual, or group, and God. The creation of a quiet space

where one can be alone with God. The inner stillness in which God can speak, and an openness to God through which he can pour the gifts of his Spirit.

Meditation directs the mind away from self, and concentrates it upon God. It stops us thinking of ourselves, our difficulties, our needs, and lets the mind soar beyond all this to God. In the silence of meditation we are learning how to open our hearts to the healing power of God's love; then, because of the close link between our physical and mental states, the body responds in a variety of ways; it may be an increase in vitality, greater resistance to infection, the easing of tensions, pain or other physical disorders.[1]

I still treasure this little gem of a book, because it opened the door to a secret world that has been life changing for me and for so many others. My adventure in prayer had begun!

∞ What is Christian Meditation?

Christian meditation is a deep form of prayer that can lead to direct communion with God. It is not focused on experiences or requests, but on surrender. We are learning the simplicity of being with God.

When we emphasise experience we are in danger of developing a consumerist pick-'n'-mix spirituality, where God's presents to us matter more than his presence. Christian meditation is centred on listening to God and obeying his Word. There is no vague, unintelligible mantra spoken. We are simply following the instruction in the Bible to meditate on God's Word: 'Do not let this Book of the Law depart from your mouth; meditate on it day and night, so that you may be careful to do everything written in it. Then you will be prosperous and successful' (Joshua 1:8).

Christian meditation differs from other forms of meditation because it does not require us to empty our minds and hearts, nor does it encourage a preoccupation with self. To quote Joyce Huggett in her book *Learning the Language of Prayer*:

> Christian meditation must not be confused with yoga, Eastern meditation or transcendental meditation. For unlike these disciplines, Christian meditation engages every part of us – our mind, our emotions, our imagination, our creativity and, supremely, our will.[2]

When we meditate, we reflect on the Word of God and allow it to roll over in our minds so that we can internalise it. It's like chewing food and allowing all the nutrients from the rich feast of God's Word to be assimilated into our being. In fact, the Bible tells us that God commends those who 'chew on Scripture day and night' (Psalm 1:2 MSG).

Someone once explained the concept of meditation to me by describing a typical scene outside our city centre church – a place where people often stop to feed bread to the pigeons. 'That's like us,' she said, 'God gives us exactly what we need for each day. He feeds us individually.' This also helped to give me a fresh understanding of the meaning of the Lord's Prayer and in particular the phrase, 'Give us this day our daily bread'. This is a great place to start meditating from, by allowing the familiarity of the Lord's Prayer to percolate through our minds and hearts so that it speaks to us in new ways.

∞ Beware of Information Overload!

Try reading this:

Hitherethanksforreadingmybookitsgreattosharewithyou
mypassionforthisverypowerfulformofprayermyownjourneyi
ntoChristianmeditationhasbeenalifechangingadventurewher
eIhavelearnedhowtodrawclosetotheheartofGodandtodiscern
hisleadingformylifethisbookcomesfromthatplaceofseekingthe
Fatherspresenceandlisteningtohisvoiceandallowinghimtodire
ctmypathIpraythatyouarereallyblessedasyoubeginorcontinu
eyouradventureintoprayerbythewaydidyouknowthatmeditati
onwasanaturalstressbusterandantidepressant?someresearchst
udiesshowthatitcanevenhelpyoutolivelongermeditationisalso
anaturalantidotetoinformationoverloadsodoyourselfafavour
andtakesometimeoutwithGoditcouldbethebestinvestmentyou
evermake!

Does that paragraph give you a headache? It gave me one writing it!

But that is exactly how many of us live our lives – without a break, without punctuation, without ——————— space, ... full stops and, , , , , , , , , , commas. We're not even sure where the Capital letters go anymore because our lives are so busy that one task runs into another and another. Even taking a proper lunch break has become a thing of the past. We're in survival mode, treading water trying to keep our head above the deadlines and the ever increasing pile of work to be done. The irony is, that our culture applauds our busyness, even though it is contributing to the breakdown of our health and family life.

Information overload has created a new form of stress, and many of us dread opening our emails. Somehow, after a busy information-filled day, even reading the Bible can seem too much to cope with, and when you're tired, it's hard to concentrate.

The good news is that meditation is a great antidote to information overload. To quote a friend of mine, 'The value of meditation is that because you're not overloaded with words, it gives you space to contemplate the "gems".'

Sounds wonderful!

∞ Dialling G for God

My quiet is so regularly intruded upon by the noise of mobile phones that I have become increasingly irritated by them and the seemingly inane conversations that take place. Okay, yes I admit it, I have one too! Last year, however, whilst travelling on a train back from Scotland, my irritation turned to inspiration, and I had what Oprah Winfrey describes as 'a light bulb moment'.

When I first learned how to meditate some fourteen years ago, Joyce Huggett, my vicar's wife (and the author of *Learning the Language of Prayer*, which I quote above), spoke of tuning in to God like a radio, adjusting the dial until you could hear God speak. It was like trying to find his frequency. With the digital revolution, of course, radios rarely have dials anymore. They usually find a particular station automatically by scanning through the frequencies. So the radio metaphor has lost some of its impact. If only hearing from God were so easy!

Still, I've found that another, more recent technological device, the mobile phone, has really helped me to have a much fuller understanding of the importance of prayer and meditation in my life and to communicate this with others. Like mobile communication, our relationship with God is dynamic; it's every day, every hour, every minute, and it can be every bit as 'cool' and exciting. Wouldn't it be great if people spent as much time with God as they do making calls or sending text messages!

My first mobile phone, affectionately described as 'a brick', was not as high-tech as my new one, but that old phone gave me a lot of on-screen information and served as a reminder of six ways in which mobile communication can teach us to communicate more effectively with God.

1. Switching On

First, before you can use a mobile phone, you have to switch it on. In the same way we have to take time to switch on to God, to show our willingness to spend time with him. Just expressing to him your openness is a start, as in this simple prayer:

> Lord, help me to focus on you,
> as we spend time together today.
> Renew my mind and help me to let go
> of all the clutter that gets in the way.

2. Registering

Next, my mobile phone has to take a few seconds to register its connection to the phone system, which is a reminder to me to acknowledge my own connectedness to God. You need to admit your dependence on that connection:

> Lord, you are my Father and Saviour,
> Creator and Lord
> Apart from you
> I can do
> nothing.

3. Searching

Then my mobile phone screen tells me that it is searching for the particular person I am trying to call. It is trying to find his or her signal. This is like tuning in to God's presence, taking time just to be quiet and hear that 'still small voice' of God. But if I hear nothing, I have not failed, because even wasting time with the one we love is valuable. In fact, it's at the heart of prayer. As lovers grow in intimacy, words become unnecessary, and, to quote one retreatant, 'Silence says all'. We don't spend time with God for what we get from him. Wasting time with God is always an investment. One day we will have nothing but time to spend with God – so our quiet times and Sabbath rests now are simply preparation for heaven.

4. Signal Strength Low

Tiredness, stress, anxiety, illness, relationship difficulties, interruptions, children screaming in another room will interfere with our ability to focus on God. Somehow, we have to learn either how to ignore the internal and external noises or how to incorporate them in such a way that they no longer become a distraction.

5. Battery Low

What a wonderful reminder *battery low* is. My mobile phone will only function for twenty-four hours before it displays this warning. At that point I have to recharge its batteries by plugging it into an electricity source.

In the same way we have to keep coming back to base, returning to our Source, which is God. This is exactly what Jesus did when he took time out to be with his Father: 'After leaving them, he [Jesus] went up on a mountainside to pray' (Mark 6:46).

The pattern of ministering and withdrawal, giving out and then receiving, is biblical. It was modelled by Jesus, and Jesus encouraged his disciples to adopt this same pattern. 'Then, because so many people were coming and going that they did not even have a chance to eat, he said to them "Come with me by yourselves to a quiet place and get some rest"' (Mark 6:31).

We too can be recharged, re-energised and refocused by returning to base and taking time out with our Father.

6. Charging complete . . .

What a lovely thought! When our charging is complete, we are ready to face anything!

∞ So What Does the Bible Tell Us to Meditate On?

But the question arises: What exactly should we meditate on? What thoughts should we bring to mind? Well, the Bible gives us guidance on this:

God's Word

> I am awake before the cry of the watchman,
> that I may meditate on Your word. (Psalm 119:148 AMP)

God's Law and Commands

> Oh, how I love your law!
> I meditate on it all day long. (Psalm 119:97)

God's Creation

> When I consider your heavens,
> the work of your fingers,
> the moon and the stars,
> which you have set in place ... (Psalm 8:3)

God's Miracles and Mighty Deeds

> I will meditate on your works
> and consider all your mighty deeds. (Psalm 77:12)

God's Unfailing Love

> Within your temple, O God,
> we meditate on your unfailing love. (Psalm 48:9)

God's Promises

> ... that I may meditate on your promises. (Psalm 119:148 AMP)

CHAPTER 2

Why Meditate?

The Old Testament refers to meditation fifty-eight times, and many of the Psalms almost sing with the word.

The word *meditate* first appears in Genesis – when Isaac is described as going 'out to the field one evening to meditate' (Genesis 24:63). Then in the book of Joshua, God commands Joshua to meditate on his Word. 'Do not let this Book of the Law depart from your mouth; meditate on it day and night, so that you may be careful to do everything written in it. Then you will be prosperous and successful' (Joshua 1:8).

This commandment to meditate on God's Word is still relevant to us today. As Paul says in Colossians: 'Let the word of Christ dwell in you richly as you teach and admonish one another with all wisdom, and as you sing psalms, hymns and spiritual songs with gratitude in your hearts to God' (3:16).

Or, to quote the Reverend Dr John Stott – a leading English theologian and writer – 'God's people grow mainly by the Word of God. As Jesus said, quoting from Deuteronomy, "human beings do not live by bread only, but by every word from the mouth of God". It is the Word of God that matures the people of God.'[3]

The purpose of the Word of God is to help us know the God of the Word. Meditation helps me to 'know' God, and that 'knowing' leads to greater intimacy with him. My favourite Scripture on meditation is found at the very beginning of the Psalms. Psalm 1 succinctly sums up the benefits of meditation:

> Blessed is the man . . .
> [whose] delight is in the law of the Lord,
> and on his law he meditates day and night.
> He is like a tree planted by streams of water,
> which yields its fruit in season
> and whose leaf does not wither.
> Whatever he does prospers. (Psalm 1:1–3)

I love that image of the tree. When I meditate it's as though I am sending my roots down deeper into the rich soil of God's love, and it is there that I meet with him and am deeply fed and nourished. It's from this place of intimacy and deep refreshment that I gain inner strength, stability and clarity of vision. Meditation also protects my health and well being, ensuring that I have the resources I need to serve God. As Proverbs says: 'Don't lose sight of my words. Let them penetrate deep within your heart, for they bring life and radiant health to anyone who discovers their meaning' (4:21–22 NLT).

Ten Reasons People Give for Not Meditating

- 'It's not biblical.'
- 'I don't have time.'
- 'I'd fall asleep.'

- 'It would take too long to learn how to meditate.'
- 'It's for monks and mystics isn't it, not for people like me?'
- 'God never speaks to me.'
- 'I wouldn't know how or where to start.'
- 'I'm not very good at using my imagination.'
- 'It's not concrete enough.'
- 'I can't concentrate.'

∞ Some More Benefits:

There are so many great reasons to meditate. Consider these others, for instance:

- Meditating on God's Word helps us to know God and his truth, and to apply that truth to our lives. It also helps us to know the character of Christ so that we can become more Christlike. Paul said that it was his determined purpose to *know* Christ and that is our purpose too. 'All I want is to know Christ and the power that raised him to life' (Philippians 3:10 CEV).

- Meditating on God's Word feeds and strengthens us . . . 'Man does not live on bread alone but on every word that comes from the mouth of the Lord' (Deuteronomy 8:3).

- As we continue to meditate on God's Word it helps us to understand it as well as memorise it. 'The entrance of your words gives light; it gives understanding to the simple' (Psalm 119:130).

- When we meditate, the 'eyes of our heart' are opened so that we can be led by God. Just like Elijah in the wilderness, we become sensitive to that 'still small voice' directing our path. 'Your word is a lamp to my feet and a light for my path' (Psalm 119:105).

- Meditation helps us to know that our true identity is in Christ. 'I have been crucified with Christ and I no longer live, but Christ lives in me' (Galatians 2:20).

- As we meditate on God's Word we are cleansed and purified. 'You are cleansed and pruned already, because of the word which I have given you [the teachings I have discussed with you]' (John 15:3 AMP).

- When we meditate on God's Word our faith is built up. 'Consequently, faith comes from hearing the message, and the message is heard through the word of Christ' (Romans 10:17).

- Meditating on God's Word is healing. God can heal us directly through his Word as Psalm 107 reminds us. 'He sent forth his word and healed them' (Psalm 107:20).

- Meditating on God's Word helps us to resist the devil and stand firm because the Word has become part of our spiritual armour. 'Take the helmet of salvation and the sword of the Spirit, which is the word of God' (Ephesians 6:17). When Jesus was tempted by Satan in the desert his weapon was the Word. Jesus said 'It is written: "Man does not live on bread alone, but on every word that comes from the mouth of God"' (Matthew 4:4).

∞ Ten More Great Reasons to Meditate

Still not convinced? Then let me add ten more reasons to meditate:

- It helps us to focus on God rather than ourselves.
- It increases our awareness and appreciation of everything around us.
- It gives our lives a deeper sense of meaning and purpose.
- It encourages greater intimacy with God and others.
- It reduces anxiety, tension and stress.
- It leads to greater emotional stability.
- It relaxes the body and calms the mind.
- It helps us to accept ourselves.
- It's quick.
- It's fun!

∞ Getting to *Know* God through His Word

As you've seen from the reasons listed above, meditation goes hand-in-hand with reading the Bible, for clearly, the best way to know God intimately is to read his book. But research shows that there is a general decline in Bible reading, so perhaps this represents an opportunity for us to discover exciting new ways to engage with the Bible – ways that are more relevant to today's sound-bite technological culture. If we can find time to read and send emails, text each other, surf the web or glance at a newspaper, then we can also choose to find time to connect with God through his most sacred text – his Word.

But it requires discipline, an unpopular word in today's culture. Perhaps, instead, we should see it as an exciting privilege and ask God to help us incorporate Scripture into our daily routine. If we seek God's divine timetable for our lives, rather than our own hit and miss agenda, reading and reflecting on Scripture could become as natural as breathing. We'll hardly know that we are doing it. Engaging with the Bible does not have to feel like a chore, it can be as creative as you choose to make it, and maybe your creative approach will inspire others.

Keep trying different approaches until you find something that works for you and that fits into your lifestyle. I've given you a whole range of ideas throughout this book for you to try out, so that engaging with the Bible becomes more of an adventure than a dirge.

∞ Taking Time Out with God

Our busyness can lead to a fatigue that causes us to lose perspective and a sense of balance in our lives. Prayer and quiet times get squeezed out as other people's needs and demands crowd in.

Jesus could have healed many more people and been far busier during his relatively short period of ministry, but he chose to listen to his Father and do what he said. He regularly took quality time out to pray, which is effective time management. He frequently withdrew up a mountain or across the lake in order to get away from the crowds. In fact, when you next read through the Gospels, it's an interesting exercise to observe just how frequently Jesus took time out.

His ministry was punctuated by withdrawal. That was his action plan for effective ministry, so it is not surprising that he encouraged his disciples to do the same.

I love the fact that in the Psalms the Hebrew word *selah* translated as 'pause and think about these things', appears seventy-one times. It is as though the psalmists are encouraging us to find life's pauses and to reflect on God's Word. What a wonderful antidote to our busy stressful lives – finding the pauses in our day to meditate on God.

I write this at a time of great pressure in my own life, juggling many roles as a writer, speaker, retreat leader, patron of a charity, broadcaster and performer. I'm also preparing to lead meditation workshops at a major Christian conference for thousands of people. My spiritual director has commented that I seem to be trying to lead several lives at once! But my busyness is not a badge to be worn with pride, even though society seems to equate busyness with productivity and success. It's a source of concern and needs constant review.

Ask Yourself

- Are you trying to lead several lives at once? List all your different roles in life.
- Are you trying to juggle too much? Ask God to show you whether you are.

When we become too busy to take time out with God, we lose intimacy with him. When we lose intimacy with God we lose touch with ourselves and humanity. We are then more likely to operate out of our own strength rather than God's and our work or ministry may become less effective and more exhausting. If we take time to withdraw as Jesus did, our activities are much more likely to be God led rather than self driven.

∞ Asking and Listening

> Trust in the LORD with all your heart; do not depend on your own understanding. Seek his will in all you do, and he will direct your paths. (Proverbs 3:5–6 NLT)

As my own work and ministry have expanded, I've had to learn how to let go of old areas of ministry so that I can embrace new ones. But it's not easy finding out what to let go of and what new things to take on. Many people are searching for answers to their lives, but often, don't think to ask God questions.

Asking questions was an important part of Jesus' ministry. Take some time now to ask God the following questions and then write down the first things that enter your mind. In the coming weeks take time to reflect and pray about these things, perhaps discussing them with a close friend.

- Lord, are there things in my life that are no longer fruitful?
- Lord, are there any new areas that you are releasing me into?

As I asked God these questions the words 'Behold, I make all things new' (Revelation 21:5 KJV) sprang to mind. Even during the course of writing this book, God has brought about so many changes in my life and has honoured that Scripture.

Letting go can be painful and requires that we relinquish control. If we continue down a path that is no longer fruitful, however, we are wasting our time and energy, for God will always move us out of our comfort zones, forward into his purposes. Like the vine, the branches are cut back so that they can be even more fruitful. 'I am the true vine, and my Father is the gardener. He cuts away every branch of mine that doesn't produce fruit. But he trims clean every branch that does produce fruit, so that it will produce even more fruit' (John 15:1–2 CEV).

It is reassuring to know that, with God in control, perhaps we can learn how to work smarter rather than just harder.

∞ Who's in the Driving Seat – You or God?

Through sheer exhaustion Elijah said that he wanted to die. He was depressed and fed up. 'I have had enough, LORD,' he said (1 Kings 19:4).

But it is important to set this in context. Elijah had just had two great spiritual victories. The defeat of the prophets of Baal and answered prayer for rain. He was experiencing a real low after a spiritual high.

I love the gentle way God cared for Elijah. He didn't deny Elijah his feelings of exhaustion but allowed him to rest and eat. God met Elijah's needs by sending him a ministering companion in the form of an angel who told him to 'Get up and eat, for the journey is too much for you' (1 Kings 19:7).

I wonder how often you've been working so hard for God that you have overlooked your own practical needs. I have done this on many occasions, and the consequences are usually disastrous.

Once Elijah had slept, eaten, drank and rested sufficiently, he was so strengthened that he was able to travel 'forty days and forty nights until he reached Horeb, the mountain of God' (1 Kings 19:8). In the presence of God, Elijah was given his full instructions via a gentle whisper: 'Go back the way you came' (1 Kings 19:15). His provision also included a much needed attendant and successor Elisha. This passage of Scripture is a wonderful reminder that God always equips those he calls, however tough the assignment.

Try It for Yourself

- Read 1 Kings 19 and see if there are any ways that you can relate to Elijah and his experience as you read the passage.
- Do any words, ideas or phrases stand out for you? If so, ask God to show you what he might be saying to you through them. Is there anything you'd like to say to God?

I was, I thought, being 'very zealous for the Lord' (1 Kings 19:10), preparing for an Easter conference where I was to be a guest speaker. I was so busy that I didn't have time to engage with the Easter story, the most important event in the Christian calendar! Yet, when I took time to ask the above questions, God was telling me to rest. So I argued with him and said, 'But Lord, I've got to prepare for this conference and there are thousands of people coming . . . and . . . and . . .'

But God was telling me to rest, to relax and enjoy this special time. He would reveal things to me one step at a time. I was to seek him for his sake, not to gain material for my seminars or even the next book. But I didn't listen. I have such a strong tendency to be purpose-driven and goal-orientated at times that I override God and don't allow myself to be led.

Does that ever happen to you?

Next time you get carried away working for the Lord, try this reality check:

- Whose kingdom am I serving (mine or God's)?
- What is my motivation for being ... or doing ... ?

One of my recurring dreams is that I am driving a car and God is sitting in the back. On one occasion, I was sitting in the back and God was sitting in the front. Now this seemed like a considerable improvement until I realised that in the dream I was still trying to drive the car from the back seat. Presumably I either had dual controls or extendible legs!

Some months later I came across this translation of Matthew 16:24 in *The Message* and suddenly everything made sense: 'Anyone who intends to come with me has to let me lead. You're not in the driver's seat, I am.' I later spent some time meditating on Psalm 23 and wrote this personal response.

The Lord is driving the car and I'm his passenger.
We travel together at his speed,
so I don't need to worry –
We even have time to stop and enjoy the countryside!
Even though I'm very busy
His way is one of efficiency
So instead of worrying,

I'll sit back and enjoy the ride!
He'll show me how to live a more balanced life,
Then I'll really know how to enjoy myself,
because I'll be trusting in God for everything.
Meanwhile, I'll sit back and relax, because
God is in the driving seat, not me!

∞ Don't Look Down!

The book I found most helpful in 2002 was John Ortberg's *If You Want to Walk on Water You've Got to Get Out of the Boat*. The title is derived from Matthew 14, which is an excellent passage for meditation, especially if you are struggling with fear and doubt. In 2003, as I reflected back, I became aware of how often I had allowed fear and anxiety to dominate my thinking and to destabilise me. When I stare at the raging waters below, I begin to sink, because I no longer have my eyes firmly fixed on Jesus but on the problem. Fear is the great enemy of faith and one the enemy loves to exploit, so it's not surprising that the Bible tells us to 'fear not' as many as 365 times, one for each day of the year!

All of us are tempted to look down while we try to walk on the water. Which of the following reasons do you resonate with?

Tiredness and exhaustion

Comparing yourself to others

Workaholism

Busyness

Not spending enough time with God and his Word

Disputes and arguments

Unforgiveness

Doubt

Reasoning

Rejection

Betrayal

Disappointment

Health problems

Anxiety and fear

Unemployment

Self pity

Lack of faith and trust

Being out of God's timing

Allowing your past to control you

Unhealed wounds from the past

False idols – God is no longer number one in your life

Ask God to show you if there is anything causing you to sink at the moment. If there is, ask him to help you in this area and visualise yourself handing over your concerns to him as you read this Scripture. 'Casting the whole of your care [all your anxieties, all your worries, all your concerns, once and for all] on Him, for He cares for you affectionately and cares about you watchfully' (1 Peter 5:7 AMP).

You may want to pray a prayer like this: 'Lord, I give you all my worries and all my fears, knowing that as you take them from me, I can walk free.'

My New Year's resolution is to not let my feelings blur my focus. I want my faith in God to be so strong and focused that it enables me to 'water-walk' without sinking. Now as I meditate on this passage, I can see myself stepping out in trust. I visualise myself not only 'water-walking' but reaching the other side knowing that 'I can do everything with the help of Christ who gives me the strength' (Philippians 4:13 NLT). And as I do so, I walk straight into Jesus' arms.

As you read the Scripture below, try to visualise the scene and then allow yourself to step into it in your imagination. See Jesus walking on the lake and beckoning you to join him. He says to you, 'Don't worry, it's only me. You can walk on water. Just believe and you'll see. You *can* do it.' Now visualise yourself walking on the surface of the water, one step at a time. Jesus is close by with his arms outstretched towards you. Now feel the warmth of his embrace as he hugs you to himself and says, 'Well done.'

> But Jesus immediately said to them: 'Take courage! It is I. Don't be afraid.'
>
> 'Lord, if it's you,' Peter replied, 'tell me to come to you on the water.'
>
> 'Come,' he said.
>
> Then Peter got down out of the boat, walked on the water and came toward Jesus. But when he saw the wind, he was afraid and, beginning to sink, cried out, 'Lord, save me!'
>
> Immediately Jesus reached out his hand and caught him. 'You of little faith,' he said, 'why did you doubt?'
>
> And when they climbed into the boat, the wind died down. Then those who were in the boat worshipped him, saying, 'Truly you are the Son of God.' (Matthew 14:27–33 TNIV)

∞ Uncovering Hidden Depths

The times of difficulty in our lives can be a pathway to greater intimacy with Jesus. It's when I find myself in darkness and despair that God's invitation is always to go deeper into him. The Psalms cry out from the depths of despair, and yet God reaches down into that pit of darkness, promising a way out.

'Out of the Depths I cry to you, O Lord; O Lord, hear my voice . . . I wait for the Lord, my soul waits, and in his word I put my hope' (Psalm 130:1, 2, 5). Joseph in the Old Testament, named his first born son Manasseh 'because God has made me forget all my trouble'. He named his second son Ephraim 'because God has made me fruitful in the land of my suffering' (Genesis 41:51–52).

During burnout I came across the following quote by Henri Nouwen which seemed to speak to me personally.

> God is beckoning you to a greater hiddenness, do not be afraid of the invitation. Over the years you have allowed the voices that call you to action and great visibility to dominate your life. You still think, even against your own best intuitions, that you need to do things and be seen in order to follow your vocation. But you are now discovering that God's voice is saying, 'Stay home, and trust and that your life will be fruitful even when hidden . . . You have friends who know that your inner voice speaks the truth and affirm what it says. They offer you a safe space where you can let that voice become clearer and louder.'[4]

When I meditate, I try to remember the three R's with regards to Scripture – Read, Reflect, Respond – but God was giving me his own three R's:

> **Rest** in my love.
>
> **Relax** in my care.
>
> **Receive** my healing.

I also sense that God is saying, 'Liz, your life is the most important book anyone could ever read.'

∞ Beating Burnout: Let Go and Let God Lead You!

And the servant of the Lord must not strive;
but be . . . patient. (2 Timothy 2:24 KJV)

Our identity in Christ is found in what he has done for us rather than what we can do for him. Focusing on work and productivity can be a route to pride as well as stress. Jesus came to set us free from imbalance of all kinds. It's wonderful the way God allows us to work in partnership with him and chooses to fulfil his plans and purposes through us. God does not need us to fulfil his plans, however. None of us is indispensable.

Burnout is a place of spiritual and emotional bankruptcy. In burnout we have lost the ability to rest and often the ability to pray. We've lost the plot. Sometimes we can think we are relaxing when in fact we're often still running on the inside. It is, therefore, vital to spend time with God so that we can regain perspective and allow him to restore our soul. Try responding to Jesus' invitation now: 'Come to Me, all you who labour and are heavy-laden and overburdened, and I will cause you to rest. [I will ease and relieve and refresh your souls]' (Matthew 11:28 AMP).

- Spend a few minutes asking God to show you those areas of your life that are out of balance. You might find it helpful to write down the first things that come to mind.
- Each week you have 168 hours deposited in your bank account. How will you spend yours this week?
- Now ask God to show you how he would like you to spend those hours? You could be in for a surprise!

∽ The Lord is My Programmer

I received this wonderful twenty-first-century adaptation of Psalm 23 by email recently.

The Lord is my programmer, I shall not crash.
He installed His software on the hard disk of my heart;
All of His commands are user-friendly.
His directory guides me to the right choices for His name's sake.
Even though I scroll through the problems of life,
I will fear no bugs, for He is my backup.
His password protects me.
He prepares a menu before me in the presence of my enemies.
His help is only a keystroke away.
Surely goodness and mercy will follow me all the days of my life,
And my file will be merged with His and saved forever.
Amen.[5]

On one occasion when I was meditating on the Scripture 'Be still, and know that I am God' (Psalm 46:10), the words seemed to gradually change as God spoke to me: 'Liz, switch off and know that I am God.' Then the words changed again and became even more personal, 'Liz, switch off from your work and plug into me so that I can recharge you.'

God can speak to us in a variety of ways through Scripture, so it's not surprising that he speaks in a language that uses contemporary imagery like the mobile phone. I was meditating upon this Scripture again recently with regards to writing this book and I sensed God was saying 'Liz, chill out and know that I am God.' God was reminding me that despite my fears of failure, that he is in control.

∞ Purpose and Presence

We discover our destiny as we journey into God, and the closer we cling to him, the easier it will be to discern the next stage of the journey. 'I will instruct you and teach you in the way you should go' (Psalm 32:8). God's purpose for our life is dependent on God's presence. The more we crave God's presence and come to know him, the more readily we are able to discern his leading.

Paul was passionate about knowing God intimately:

'[My determined purpose is] that I may know Him [that I may progressively become more deeply and intimately acquainted with Him, perceiving and recognising and under-standing the wonders of His Person more strongly and more clearly]' (Philippians 3:10 AMP).

And David expressed his hunger for God in so many of the Psalms: 'Your love means more than life to me.' (Psalm 63:3 CEV)

Moses longed to see the face of God and it was through his life changing encounter that he was able to hear and to fulfil the plans of God. A sense of purpose and God's presence go hand-in-hand.

Jesus said, 'Go and make disciples of all nations' (Matthew 28:19). But he also said, 'I am with you always, to the very end of the age' (Matthew 28:20).

Try It for Yourself

Moses was instructed by God to record the stages of the Israelites' journeys. This provided a record of both spiritual and geographical progress (Numbers 33).

- Chart your life's journey to date with its ups and downs, making a note of key events in your life. You could represent this as a drawing using a time line, or winding path graduated in five-year blocks. You could also use different colours to represent the ups (yellow) and downs (grey-black).
- At what points in your life have you felt closest to God? You could colour these orange. At what points in your life have you felt distant from God? You could colour these brown.
- Intimacy with God is frequently forged through suffering. Has this been your experience?

∞ Spiritual Health Check

Our relationship with God needs to be real. I find it helpful to incorporate questions into my prayers so that I can evaluate where I am in terms of my relationship with him. It's a sort of spiritual health check.

You might like to try this yourself. Don't try to think too hard about any question, just simply write down the first things that come into mind. Then, over the coming weeks ask God to show you whether what you've written down is accurate.

- Where are you in your relationship with God? (You might find it helpful to visualise this physically.) Where is God in relation to where you are sitting or standing now?

- What is God saying to you at this point in your life?

- Is there anything or any person standing in the way of your relationship with God? (What or who pre-occupies your thoughts?)

- Are there any things that God is calling you to let go of?

- *Behold, I make all things new* (Revelation 21:5 KJV). Is God transforming anything in your life? Is there anything new that he is calling you to?

I asked myself this series of questions whilst writing this, and I believe God was saying to me, 'Let go and let me lead. I can do it, but you can't on your own. I've called you to work with me, not to run ahead of me.' This fits in with a picture a friend had for me some months before I became ill. She saw me running down the road distributing my books and God running behind trying to keep up!

During burnout and recovery I have felt very close to God. The pathway to God's presence is often renewed in brokenness and the intensity of my need has led to greater dependency on God. If only I was always so hungry and thirsty for God!

As I asked God to show me anything that might be standing in the way of my relationship with him, the answer came very quickly – 'workaholism'. When someone prayed for me recently, they sensed that God wanted to set me free from overwork. God was calling me to let go of work, to surrender the pressure that I had taken on regarding this book and all my other publications and release everything to him. Ironically, I have taught countless others about the importance of surrender and yet here I was holding on to work as an idol. I then asked God to show me if there were any new things he was calling me to. These new things included having fun and learning how to laugh again.

CHAPTER 3

How to Meditate

Many people associate meditation with staring at a candle for half an hour or sitting cross-legged, chanting strange things.

But in Scripture we are encouraged to 'pray continually' (1 Thessalonians 5:17). So I meditate anytime, anywhere, on the move or when stationary, on the train, at work, in a business meeting, in traffic jams, in the shower, at the gym, etc.

I've tried to incorporate prayer and meditation into my day without making a big deal of it, so that it becomes a natural part of my life. It is, of course, also important to spend quality time with God in prayer and meditation, so here are some helpful suggestions:

∞ How Long Should I Meditate?

Like any discipline, meditation takes practice. So don't try for an Olympic style meditation once a month. Little and often will result in your learning and integrating this form of prayer into the routine of your life. Initially just aim for a couple of minutes a day. You could begin by focusing on a word like *Jesus* (see 'The Jesus Prayer' later in this chapter) and co-ordinate it with your breathing; or you could focus on a short line of Scripture, such as the ones found at the end of the book. In time, meditation will become a natural part of your life and you will be enjoying the presence of God without even realising it.

∞ Preparation

Before starting, take into account these three preliminaries: comfort, posture and atmosphere. Once you have these in place, you are ready to begin.

Comfort

Warmth – If it's too warm you may fall asleep, but if it's too cold you won't be able to concentrate. When you meditate, your body temperature decreases so you're likely to need extra layers of clothing.

Space – You might want to choose a particular room or corner of a room to meditate and pray. In time it will become sacred space so that each time you return to it, you will find it easier to switch off and tune in to God.

Clothes – Choose clothes that are comfortable and warm, with socks or slipper socks in winter. If you wear layers of clothes, it is easier to adjust you body temperature accordingly.

Posture

Sit, lie, kneel or stand? Some people like to meditate using bean bags and floor cushions, or even lying on a bed. Experiment and see what works for you. Lying on floors can be draughty, so you need to take this into account. If lying on the floor hurts your back, try bending your knees to create more support for your back.

Alternatively, you might want to use a comfortable high-backed chair. A small pillow to support your neck is helpful whether sitting or lying down.

Don't worry if you fall asleep, many people do. Try propping yourself up or sitting. Some people invest in wooden prayer stools (which are rather like church kneelers); these allow you to kneel for a longer period of time because the weight is taken off your knees as you sit back on the stool.

Open posture – An open posture, with the palms of your hands facing upwards signals a readiness to receive from God. Try not to cross your legs as it tends to inhibit the flow of blood around the body.

Atmosphere

- *Noise* – Complete silence is difficult to achieve and some noise is inevitable. In time, however, you will learn how to ignore or integrate noises so that you don't notice them. Choose a quiet part of the day to meditate, so that you are less likely to be disturbed – and remember to switch phones off.

- *Light* – Subdued lighting is more relaxing. Use blinds to screen strong sunlight. Candles can provide a gentle light and visual focus.

- *Visuals* – Some people find pictures, Scripture cards, flowers, natural objects, candles, etc., helpful to focus their attention, and to create a more relaxing environment.

- *Prayer* – There is nothing like prayer to change the atmosphere of a room. So have a special place to pray and meditate even if it is only the corner of a room or a special chair. I have a reclining chair and footstool, and every time I sit in that chair it seems to prompt me to pray. In time your place of prayer and meditation will become as inviting as stepping into a warm bath.

- *Music* – Many people find music relaxing. It also provides an appropriate focus and can help cover up distracting noises.

∞ Practice

With those preliminaries in place, you are ready to begin your meditation. The first things you need to focus on are . . .

Becoming Still

The Good News Bible translates Psalm 46:10 as 'Stop fighting and know that I am God', rather than 'Be still and know that I am God'. It certainly is a struggle to switch off from the busyness of life, and plug in to God. I usually find that music helps me to relax, or focusing on my breathing. Distractions, to do lists, anxiety and mind-chatter are the norm when meditating, so don't think you've failed before you've even started! Have a note pad at hand to jot important things down to help your concentration.

If you're still struggling to switch off, you could imagine that you have a special volume control dial on the side of your head and visualise yourself turning down the noise and mind-chatter as you rotate the dial. I know it sounds strange, but I find this is a helpful technique.

Breathing

It has been said that the art of relaxation is concentration. As we concentrate on our breathing, it helps us to take our minds off other preoccupations and focus them on God who breathes life into all creation.

Try this simple breathing exercise to get you started:

- Inhale 1, 2 . . .
- hold 1, 2
- Exhale 1, 2, 3, 4 . . .
- Repeat several times
- Inhale 1, 2, 3 . . .
- hold 1, 2, 3
- Exhale 1, 2, 3, 4, 5, 6 . . .
- Repeat several times

Now try breathing 'in the name of Jesus' as outlined below.

The Jesus Prayer

The Jesus Prayer is an ancient prayer that comes in many forms, the most famous of which is 'Lord Jesus, have mercy upon me, a sinner'. But an even simpler form is to repeat the name of Jesus.

Spend a short time focusing on the rhythm of your breathing, and then repeat the name *Jesus* silently to yourself allowing the Holy Spirit to breathe new life into you. You could inhale 'Je' and exhale 'sus', or say Jesus during or after exhalation.

As we focus on Jesus in this way, we are reminded that he is our hope, our peace, our joy, our rock and our salvation. It is the name of Jesus that is at the heart of our prayers ... our lives ... our work ... our ministry ... our leisure ... our laughter ... and our sorrow. Our whole being is dependent on Jesus.

Repeating the name of Jesus to myself as a form of prayer is now so familiar to me that I'm not sure how many times a day I am praying it. I've managed to integrate it into my daily routine no matter what I'm doing, where I'm going or how I'm feeling. It's my ongoing prayer and a real stress buster, helping me to keep my eyes firmly fixed on Jesus. I also find that it helps override my tendency to worry and replay negative conversations and situations in my mind. It is especially helpful when I have problems sleeping.

∞ If You Can Worry You Can Meditate!

Both John Ortberg in his book *If You Want to Walk on Water* and Rick Warren in *The Purpose-Driven Life* mention the importance of meditation, commenting that if you can worry you can meditate. In many ways that is true. As a dog refuses to let go of a bone, so we often rehearse, replay and review our worries and fears until they loom so large that we are unable to let go of them. It's as though our video replay button is stuck. If only we were so tenacious about Scripture! This replaying and reviewing of Scripture is at the heart of meditation. It's far more productive to rehearse Scripture than fear and anxiety. So next time you feel yourself getting wound up, press the pause button or even the stop button in your mind and superimpose God's promises over your fears.

∞ Getting Started

I have approach-avoidance conflict with my Bible. I'm hungry to consume it all, but I don't know how to, and when I try to do too much, it overwhelms me and I get indigestion! I've never been able to engage with daily Bible Reading notes and carried around this sense of failure and guilt with me for many years.

Now, however, I simply accept that this approach doesn't work for me. I usually find Bible notes difficult to relate to as Scripture is often filtered through the writers' experience, and often I can't relate to that experience and would rather approach Scripture directly. Perhaps too, I feel a slight sense of rebellion stirring, because it reminds me of homework!

I prefer to go directly to God and ask him to reveal the meaning of Scripture to me through the Holy Spirit. I love the disciples' response to Jesus shortly after he appeared to them on the road to Emmaus. 'Were not our hearts burning within us while he talked with us on the road and opened the Scriptures to us' (Luke 24:32). This has been my prayer as I've wrestled with the difficulty of understanding the Bible across the years.

I'm a sound bite person, with a short memory and so God has opened Scripture to me in a way that suits my attention span but also meets my desire for intimacy. I find that once I am able to digest small chunks of Scripture it stirs my interest to read more.

∾ Listening to God

> My sheep hear my voice; I know them,
> and they follow me. (John 10:27)

Spending time with some of my friends and their mobile phones has become a source of real irritation to me. Suddenly there is a third party in the conversation, and I wonder whether they actually want to listen to or spend time with me. Perhaps they would prefer to be with the person they are talking to – or texting. Even answering the phone in the middle of a conversation no longer seems to necessitate an apology; such is our addiction to mobile communication.

But God gives us his full attention. He speaks to us and he wants to be heard. That is why he gave us the Bible.

When some people say that they can't hear God, what they often mean is that they are not willing to take the time to learn how to listen. In our instant culture, we expect instant results, even with God! But it takes time to familiarise ourselves with God's voice. The book of Revelation reminds us that it is not enough to have ears to hear, we need to use them (Revelation 13:9). Listening requires vulnerability, availability and openness. We surrender ourselves, our ambitions, our schedules and our drives to God and submit to his divine plan for our life. In order to fulfil God's call on our lives we need to create space to listen to him.

Hannah dedicated her young son Samuel to serve God. When God called Samuel by name, his response was, 'Speak, for your servant is listening' (1 Samuel 3:10).

You might like to pray this prayer:

> Lord, open my life to your leading
> And my lips to speak your truth.
> Open my eyes to your presence
> And my ears to your voice.
> Open my mind to your Word
> And my heart to your love.

It is as God reveals himself to us through his Word that we become more able to hear him speaking into our lives. Sometimes we may prefer not to listen as God reveals our motives and ambitions, as well as our weaknesses and sin. Jesus, however, also tells us that 'everyone who hears these words of mine and puts them into practice is like a wise man who built his house on the rock' (Matthew 7:24).

Some people really struggle to hear God, but I believe that if we are really passionate about hearing God, then we will. The more we respond to the promptings of the Holy Spirit the easier it becomes to hear those promptings again. Each time we fail to recognise those promptings, or choose to ignore them, the harder it is to hear God next time.

How Meditation Was a Pathway to My Healing

When I was ill with ME fourteen years ago now, I heard an almost audible voice answering my prayer of desperation for healing. Some months earlier, I had begun to meditate using Joyce Huggett's book *Open to God*. Not only was she a best-selling author at the time, she was also my vicar's wife. I didn't understand the book and knew nothing about meditation, but I did try some of the exercises.

I assumed that I had failed miserably with these meditations, but then I became aware of God speaking to me. He was telling me that he was going to heal me of ME and that I should ask Joyce to pray with me. I thought I was going mad because I was now hearing voices! This was the first time I'd ever heard God speak to me, or was it the first time I'd really listened. God's suggestion really embarrassed me, however, because I didn't know Joyce very well and I'd put her on some kind of spiritual pedestal.

As my condition continued to deteriorate, I also sensed that God was telling me to go on our church's annual weekend away. I thought this was a ridiculous suggestion, as I wasn't well enough and would simply spend the whole weekend in bed. Still, I obeyed that prompting and attended Joyce's prayer session on 'Tuning In to God'.

As she encouraged us to tune in to what God was saying to us and tune out any unwelcome interference, I could hear God saying very loudly, 'You've suffered long enough, I'm going to heal you of ME so that you can go out and spread the Word. Ask Joyce to pray for you.' Again, I was embarrassed and daren't approach her through fear of rejection.

The next day I attended Joyce's second session on prayer and God was saying the same thing again, but this time even louder. At the end of the session I went forward and explained to Joyce what I believed God had been saying to me. Fortunately, Joyce was more than willing to pray with me.

I was healed instantly, but more importantly I experienced the loving presence of God in such an amazingly tangible way that day that I have not been the same since. I could never doubt the existence of God again, nor the healing power of the Holy Spirit.

Shortly after my healing I sensed God was saying, 'You'll write a book and it will be called *Can God Help M.E?*' This communication from God was so clear that I never doubted I would one day write a book to help other sufferers, even though I'd never had any aspirations to be a writer. In 1997, six years after my healing from ME, my writing ministry began and *Can God Help M.E?* was published. This book still continues to give hope to thousands of sufferers and their carers. Some sufferers have even been healed through reading it and others have become Christians.

After I led my first retreat for ME sufferers in 1996, God seemed to be saying, 'Feed my lambs', and I have since gone on to produce books, tapes and CDs for people who are suffering through illness, pain and loss. Some of my publications have even gone into hospices for the terminally ill as well as prisons.

As I write this, I am moved to tears at the amazing way God has worked in my life, releasing me from captivity and setting me free to serve others. What a privilege. What an awesome God we serve.

So do I still hear God as clearly now? Well, in those early days I was a fairly new Christian, and so his voice though rare, seemed louder and clearer. Now I am more aware of the Holy Spirit's nudges, but have to work harder at listening and need to pray carefully about what God might be saying to me. But this is a sign of growing spiritual maturity. I no longer need to be bottle fed.

∞ So How Do You Know if You've Heard from God?

The simple answer is you don't, but often the answers to your questions are so extraordinary that it seems as though these thoughts can only come from God.

I usually ask myself if what I've heard is consistent with the Bible and Christ's teaching. Is it moral, legal, ethical, loving? Is it confirmed by other mature Christians I know? I also tend to get a strong sense whether something is right or not, and then I ask God for confirmation.

A year before I was healed of ME the words of Isaiah 35 seemed to speak right into my spirit. It was as though God were speaking to me personally, and promising that he would 'come to my rescue'. A year later I was healed of ME and the first thing I did was 'leap and dance' (Isaiah 35:6 GNB). God is faithful to keep his promises.

But another important aspect of this question is to ask yourself: What is my heart's desire?

Ask Yourself

What is your heart's desire?

Jesus never made a decision without referring to his Father; 'He is able to do only what He sees the Father doing' (John 5:19 AMP). Take some time now to reflect on this question and then as you pray offer your thoughts to God. 'Lord show me your purposes for my life and lead me in the way I should go, because that is the way of efficiency and love.'

∞ Exploring Hidden Depths

One of the most moving works of sacred art that I have seen is Holman Hunt's remarkable painting *The Light of the World*. The picture is based on this well known Scripture in Revelation: 'Behold, I stand at the door and knock; if anyone hears and listens to and heeds My voice and opens the door, I will come in to him and will eat with him, and he [will eat] with Me' (Revelation 3:20 AMP). In the painting, the doorway is overgrown with weeds and no handle is visible. Jesus knocks gently at the door, but the handle is on the inside. So we have a choice whether to open it or not.

Do you feel able to allow God through his Holy Spirit, to enter every corner of your life, or are there still parts you want to conceal? Are there any rooms that you would deny him access to? In a sense, these are the doorways that have become overgrown with weeds. But God tells us to 'plough up the hard ground of your hearts!' (Jeremiah 4:3 NLT). Anything we hold on to can be a barrier to intimacy with God. Intimacy requires surrender, vulnerability and openness.

Try It for Yourself

- On a scale of 1–10, how open-hearted are you to God?
- Which compartments of your heart remain closed, denying God access?
- Ask God to show you if there is anything you are holding on to – anger, pain, fear, unforgiveness, resentment, jealousy, busyness, work etc?

∾ Open to God

To fully open our hearts to God, we need to keep surrendering control. Often, we think that we have let go when we are really still in control. This ancient prayer by Charles de Foucauld makes a wonderful meditation. Try reciting it aloud initially. Then you might like to try reflecting on just one line at a time offering it as a personal prayer of surrender, submission and openness to God. It's quite a challenge!

> Father,
> I abandon myself into your hands;
> do with me what you will.
> Whatever you may do, I thank you:
> I am ready for all. I accept all.
> Let only your will be done in me,
> and in all your creatures.
> I wish no more than this, O Lord.

> Into your hands I commend my soul;
> I offer it to you with all the love of my heart,
> for I love you, Lord,
> and so need to give myself,
> to surrender myself into your hands,
> without reserve,
> and with boundless confidence,
> for you are my Father.[6]

To help you engage with this prayer, try asking yourself this series of questions:

- In what ways do I see God as *my Father*?
- Where can I see signs of God's love in my life?
- Am I willing to surrender *all* control to God and let him lead? Can I pray the prayer 'I surrender myself to you without reserve'?
- Am I really thankful for *whatever* God does in my life good or bad?
- Am I willing to let God's will prevail totally over mine?
- How much of myself am I willing to surrender to God on a scale of 1–10 (where 10 is total surrender)?
- How much do I trust God on a scale of 1–10?
- How much do I love God on a scale of 1–10?

∞ A Love Letter from God

The greatest gift we can give God is not performance related but heart related. Our true identity is in God and as we believe and receive the gift of God's unconditional love for us, we are free to offer that gift to others and can venture along any pathway and feel secure.

Spend some time now reflecting on this rich love letter from God your Father. You might want to insert your name.

Love Letter from God to . . . .

My Child . . .

You may not know me, but I know everything about you
> . . . Psalm 139:1

I know when you sit down and when you rise up
> . . . Psalm 139:2

I am familiar with all your ways
> . . . Psalm 139:3

Even the very hairs on your head are numbered
> . . . Matthew 10:29-31

For you were made in my image
> . . . Genesis 1:27

In me you live and move and have your being
> . . . Acts 17:28

For you are my offspring
> . . . Acts 17:28

I knew you even before you were conceived
> . . . Jeremiah 1:4-5

I chose you when I planned creation
... Ephesians 1:11-12

You were not a mistake, for all your days are written in my book
... Psalm 139:15-16

I determined the exact time of your birth and where you would live
... Acts 17:26

You are fearfully and wonderfully made
... Psalm 139:14

I knit you together in your mother's womb
... Psalm 139:13

And brought you forth on the day you were born
... Psalm 71:6

I have been misrepresented by those who don't know me
... John 8:41-44

I am not distant and angry, but am the complete expression of love
... 1 John 4:16

And it is my desire to lavish my love on you
... 1 John 3:1

Simply because you are my child and I am your Father
... 1 John 3:1

I offer you more than your earthly father ever could
... Matthew 7:11

For I am the perfect Father
... Matthew 5:48

Every good gift that you receive comes from my hand

     . . . James 1:17

For I am your provider and I meet all your needs

     . . . Matthew 6:31-33

My plan for your future has always been filled with hope

     . . . Jeremiah 29:11

Because I love you with an everlasting love

     . . . Jeremiah 31:3

My thoughts toward you are countless as the sand on the seashore

     . . . Psalm 139:17-18

And I rejoice over you with singing

     . . . Zephaniah 3:17

I will never stop doing good to you

     . . . Jeremiah 32:40

For you are my treasured possession

     . . . Exodus 19:5

I desire to establish you with all my heart and all my soul

     . . . Jeremiah 32:41

And I want to show you great and marvelous things

     . . . Jeremiah 33:3

If you seek me with all your heart, you will find me

     . . . Deuteronomy 4:29

Delight in me and I will give you the desires of your heart

     . . . Psalm 37:4

For it is I who gave you those desires

     . . . Philippians 2:13

I am able to do more for you than you could possibly imagine
... Ephesians 3:20

For I am your greatest encourager
... 2 Thessalonians 2:16-17

I am also the Father who comforts you in all your troubles
... 2 Corinthians 1:3-4

When you are brokenhearted, I am close to you
... Psalm 34:18

As a shepherd carries a lamb, I have carried you close to my heart
... Isaiah 40:11

One day I will wipe away every tear from your eyes
... Revelation 21:3-4

And I'll take away all the pain you have suffered on this earth
... Revelation 21:3-4

I am your Father, and I love you even as I love my son, Jesus
... John 17:23

For in Jesus, my love for you is revealed
... John 17:26

He is the exact representation of my being
... Hebrews 1:3

He came to demonstrate that I am for you, not against you
... Romans 8:31

And to tell you that I am not counting your sins
... 2 Corinthians 5:18-19

Jesus died so that you and I could be reconciled
... 2 Corinthians 5:18-19

His death was the ultimate expression of my love for you

... 1 John 4:10

I gave up everything I loved that I might gain your love

... Romans 8:31-32

If you receive the gift of my son Jesus, you receive me

... 1 John 2:23

And nothing will ever separate you from my love again

... Romans 8:38-39

Come home and I'll throw the biggest party heaven has ever seen

... Luke 15:7

I have always been Father, and will always be Father

... Ephesians 3:14-15

My question is . . . Will you be my child?

... John 1:12-13

I am waiting for you

... Luke 15:11-32

Love, Your Dad. Almighty God[7]

You might want to revisit this rich banquet of Scripture repeatedly, perhaps focusing on a different line each day. Digesting Biblical truth in this way will help you to grow spiritually and emotionally. When you know who you really are in God and how much you mean to him, you're less likely to fill 'emotional holes' with other things.

∞ Busy or Listening? – Mary and Martha

Are you too busy to take time to listen to others, or to God?

Often the greatest gift that we can give people is to take the time to listen to them. Listening tells a person that they matter, that they are valuable. How much more important then, is it to spend quality time with God, even if we think we're too busy working *for* God to spend time *with* him! This tension is wonderfully illustrated in the story of Mary and Martha when their friend Jesus comes to visit them.

What would your reaction be if Jesus came to visit you?

Imagine Jesus knocking on your door now. What would be your immediate reaction? Would you rush round clearing up? Or would you invite him in immediately? Which part of the house would you show him in to? What would your first words to him be? Would you make him a drink, or cook him a meal, or just sit and chat?

Now as you read the Scripture below, imagine yourself stepping inside the house of Mary and Martha.

> As Jesus and his disciples were on their way, he came to a village where a woman named Martha opened her home to him. She had a sister called Mary, who sat at the Lord's feet listening to what he said. But Martha was distracted by all preparations that had to be made. She came to him and asked, 'Lord, don't you care that my sister has left me to do the work for myself? Tell her to help me!'
>
> 'Martha, Martha,' the Lord answered, 'you are worried and upset about many things, but few things are needed – or indeed only one. Mary has chosen what is better, and it will not be taken away from her.' (Luke 10:38–42 TNIV)

As you read this Scripture again, try to imagine that you are Martha busy preparing, while Mary sits there doing nothing. How does that make you feel? What do you need to get on with? Are you calm or stressed as you rush around preparing? What might Jesus say to you?

The second time you reflect on this Scripture you might like to imagine that you are Mary. The contrast will be marked as you sit listening to Jesus and enjoying his company. Are you able to fully enjoy Jesus' company or are you distracted by Martha-like thoughts and preoccupations. If so, write these things down and try again to focus on Jesus. Visualise yourself sitting next to him. What are you sitting on, or are you kneeling? Where is Jesus sitting? Is he sitting on your right or left? What is he wearing? What is he saying? Is there anything you'd like to ask him? Is there anything you would like to say to Martha? How does your time with Jesus end?

∞ Don't Compare Yourself with Others

There is a great temptation in Christian ministry to compare oneself with high flyers who seem to be like Christian superstars with boundless energy, talent, love and patience and who somehow also juggle a large family. Whenever I compare myself to others, it is usually disastrous. I feel inadequate and insignificant.

But that little I have to offer God is precious and unique and so means everything to God. He hasn't called me to be someone else, but to be uniquely myself. While others seem to be speeding down the fast lane, I've been chugging along country lanes recently. It's not very glamorous, but the view is magnificent.

Fortunately, God does not measure our output and performance level, but monitors our heart. I've come to accept that energy is also a gift from God, and we are all blessed with different amounts. God promises to equip those he calls, so I don't need to worry. His strength is made perfect in my weakness (2 Corinthians 12:9).

Serving God is not a competition. In fact, comparing ourselves to other people can distract us from the uniqueness of our call, as we are side-tracked into believing that we should be more like them. A friend of mine reminded me of this recently by saying, 'Liz you're not called to be Christine-like, you're called to be Christlike!' I was delighted to read in the Psalms that God's 'pleasure is not in the strength of the horse ... the LORD delights in those who fear him, who put their hope in his unfailing love' (Psalm 147:10–11).

Ask Yourself

- Is there anyone you are comparing yourself to?
- And if so, why?

I find the parable of the five loaves and two fishes particularly encouraging because it helps me to realise that whatever I bring to the table, God multiplies it. My little becomes much in his hands. As children of God we are called to walk in the freedom of who we are, to be uniquely ourselves. As you meditate on the feeding of the five thousand, imagine yourself giving to God your lunchbox for the day. Lord, I give all that I have and all that I am to you.

> As evening approached, the disciples came to him and said, 'This is a remote place, and it's already getting late. Send the crowds away, so they can go to the villages and buy themselves some food.'
>
> Jesus replied, 'They do not need to go away. You give them something to eat.'
>
> 'We have here only five loaves of bread and two fish,' they answered.
>
> 'Bring them here to me,' he said. And he directed the people to sit down on the grass. Taking the five loaves and two fish and looking up to heaven, he gave thanks and broke the loaves. Then he gave them to the disciples, and the disciples gave them to the people. They all ate and were satisfied, and the disciples picked up twelve basketfuls of broken pieces that were left over. The number of those who ate was about five thousand men, besides women and children. (Matthew 14:15–21 TNIV)

∞ Receiving God's Love

When you've suffered abuse or neglect in some area of your life, it is much harder to trust God and to relate to him intimately. Any form of abuse is an abomination to God and he promises his healing as well as justice.

There are times when it is important to focus on God not only as a Father but as a Mother and even a Lover, traditions of Christian thought and worship that are nearly as old as the church itself. Let us consider them here.

God as Father

There are some wonderful references in the Bible to God being our loving Father. Shortly after my father died ten years ago, I experienced the reality of God as my Father. I felt so alone because I admired and relied on my father so much. His courageous attitude toward terminal cancer inspired my search for God.

Shortly afterwards, I was visiting a missionary friend in Toronto at a time when the Toronto Blessing was much talked about. So I decided to visit the Toronto Airport Christian Fellowship. Amazing things seemed to be happening there at that time, and although the service seemed somewhat unconventional, there was a real sense of God's presence. I found myself quietly in tears as my grief rose to the surface. I told God exactly how I felt – abandoned, lost and fatherless, like an orphan. But then I received such love and comfort from God, as though he were comforting me personally. He said to me, 'You're not fatherless, I'm your Father.'

A great deal of healing took place that evening and I have not needed to grieve for my father in the same way since, now I know that God *is* my Father. When I returned to England, my car had been vandalised and the word *bastard* scraped into the paintwork in large capital letters! This enemy attack on my car, upsetting though it was, only underlined the significance and importance of that special encounter with God.

God as Mother

> Behold, I will extend peace to her like a river . . .
> As one whom his mother comforts, so I will comfort you.
> (Isaiah 66:12,13 AMP)

Our relationship with our mother is a vital one which helps to establish our identity and sense of worth. But some of us may not have felt nurtured and cherished by them and this can lead to low self-esteem. That deep need can be met in God, however, as I also discovered.

God promises to provide everything we need and is faithful to that promise. During the six months while I was ill with burnout, God was revealing that aspect of his nature to me. Sometimes this motherly love came through other people and at other times, directly from God. I sensed his loving companionship alongside me as I struggled to sleep at night. Sometimes I felt his motherly presence comforting me as I woke up in his arms, my head against his chest. At first I was alarmed, because I had not experienced this aspect of God's love before, but then I received an email from a friend:

> Now is the time that God is holding you in the depths of himself. He is nourishing you so that you can rest and grow. All you have to do is to be passive, to receive and to be nourished. I also had the sense that although God is our Father God, He is wanting to pour out his 'maternal love' to you at the moment. It's a tender, gentle, nourishing love. Having received this love, you in turn will grow to be more comfortable, more at ease with those parts of yourself that feel tender and vulnerable.

There are many references to the motherly qualities of God in the Bible. The gospel of John describes Jesus as being 'in the bosom [in the intimate presence] of the Father' (John 1:18). That was his spiritual home, and it is ours too.

> I do not concern myself with great matters . . . but I have stilled myself and quietened my soul; like a weaned child with its mother, like a weaned child is my soul within me.
> (Psalm 131:1–2 NIV)

God as Lover

In the past six months, God has been wooing me into a place of greater intimacy. He had my full attention because I was unable to work. But that is the place God is calling us to, all of the time.

I used to avoid reading Song of Songs because I found it shocking. I could hardly believe that it was part of the Bible because it was so sensual and sexual. But poetry is the language of lovers and we too can experience unfathomable depths of intimacy with God.

Our 'determined purpose' like Paul is to 'know Him' to 'progressively become more deeply and intimately acquainted with Him' (Philippians 3:10 AMP).

In 1 Samuel, it says that the Lord sought 'a man after his own heart' and that man was David (1 Samuel 13:14). David desired God above everything else. He said, 'The one thing I want from God, the thing I seek most of all, is the privilege of meditating in his Temple, living in his presence every day of my life, delighting in his incomparable perfections and glory' (Psalm 27:4 LB).

If we want to be radical Christians making a difference for the kingdom, then we too need to be passionate about spending time with God.

> My heart has heard you say, 'Come and talk with me.' And my heart responds, 'LORD, I am coming.' (Psalm 27:8 NLT)

Ask Yourself

How strong is your desire to spend time with God? Rate your answer on a scale of 1–10, where 10 is your absolute desire and 0 is where your desire has died. If you long to spend time with God but don't know how to fit quality time into your busy lifestyle, ask God to help you. And if your desire has died, ask him to renew and restore that desire in you.

∞ The Vine – a Picture of Intimacy

The image of 'the Vine' in John 15 is a wonderful picture of divine union with God, and yet it is so easy to read this metaphor in Scripture and view it solely in terms of productivity. But this image is not meant to be a guide on how-to-be-more-productive-for-God; rather, it focuses on the importance of intimacy *with* God, being 'vitally united' as the *Amplified Bible* refers to it.

The picture of the Vine is one of divine union, a oneness with God, and it is from that place of intimacy that fruitful service flows. Each branch and shoot is an extension of the main branch. Without that vital union with God through

Jesus Christ, we are reminded that we can do nothing. 'However, apart from Me [cut off from vital union with Me] you can do nothing.'

Furthermore, if we are vitally united to God and rooted in his Word, we can ask for anything and it will happen. 'If you live in Me [abide vitally united to Me], and My words remain in you and continue to live in your hearts, ask whatever you will, and it shall be done for you.'

A friend of mine felt that God had given her a 'picture' of a garden. In the garden were some beautiful trees but few flowers. Next to her, was a large rotting pile of debris with dead leaves and broken and discarded branches. She asked God to show her what this picture meant. He replied, 'The trees and the flowers represent all the things I have called you to do, but the pile of debris represents all the works I haven't authorised.'

Sometime later I read the following in a friend's prayer letter: 'Satan may not be able to entice you to stumble through the obvious sins, but if he can, he will entice you to overextend yourself, or to be drawn into doing uncommanded works. If you do so, you will be vulnerable to his attacks and forfeit the covering of the Lord's protection.'

Spend some time now reflecting on the passage of 'the Vine'. Read it slowly several times and note down or highlight any words, phrases or ideas that particularly grab your attention. Then spend some time in prayer asking God to show you what he might be saying to you through it.

> I am the True Vine, and My Father is the Vinedresser. Any branch in Me that does not bear fruit [that stops bearing] He cuts away [trims off, takes away]; and He cleanses

and repeatedly prunes every branch that continues to bear fruit, to make it bear more and richer and more excellent fruit.

You are cleansed and pruned already because of the word which I have given you [the teachings I have discussed with you]. Dwell in Me, and I will dwell in you. [Live in Me, and I will live in you.] Just as no branch can bear fruit of itself without abiding in [being vitally united to] the vine, neither can you bear fruit unless you abide in Me.

I am the Vine; you are the branches. Whoever lives in Me and I in him bears much [abundant] fruit. However, apart from Me [cut off from vital union with Me] you can do nothing.

If a person does not dwell in Me, he is thrown out like a [broken-off] branch and withers; such branches are gathered up and thrown into the fire, and they are burned. If you live in Me [abide vitally united to Me], and My words remain in you and continue to live in your hearts, ask whatever you will, and it shall be done for you.

When you bear [produce] much fruit, My Father is honoured and glorified, and you show and prove yourselves to be true followers of Mine.

I have loved you, [just] as the Father has loved Me; abide in My love [continue in his love with Me].

If you keep My commandments [if you continue to obey My instructions], you will abide in My love and live on in it, just as I have obeyed My Father's commandments and live on in His love.

I have told you these things, that My joy and delight may be in you, and that your joy and gladness may be of full measure and complete and overflowing. (John 15:1–11 AMP)

As I meditated on this passage again recently, the truth of 'I have loved you, [just] as the Father has loved Me; abide in My love [continue in his love with Me]' really hit me. In Jesus, we have access to the same depth of love and intimacy that he shares with his Father. Wow, now that is awesome.

∞ The Power of Forgiveness

The real test of love is forgiveness. It's easy to love those who love and accept us, but much harder to love those who continually seek to undermine us whether they be members of our family or work colleagues.

Recently I had a serious argument with my mother which resulted in us both feeling hurt and angry. During that same week I saw R. T. Kendall interviewed on forgiveness on American TV. He was a talking about his bestselling book *Total Forgiveness*. He said that in his experience it is not helpful to confront people with our grievances against them, because often they don't know what we are talking about. He also said that confrontation was not necessary to the process of forgiveness and neither was their apology. He was right, the confrontation with my mother got me nowhere, it simply made her feel a failure and me a reject. So after a lot of heartache on both sides, I apologised for upsetting her.

There is no doubt that the most powerful prayers we can pray are for our enemies, because in so doing we release them as well as ourselves. God has given us grace to forgive, but we have a choice as to whether to or not. Forgiveness is a process, not a one-off event, but as we continue to forgive the pain diminishes.

Try It for Yourself

You might want to think about a relationship that is a problem for you at the moment. Now visualise a bridge and see yourself about to cross the bridge. Jesus is standing alongside you and he says, 'Are you ready to walk across now?' What is your reply? As you walk across, ask Jesus to show you how much he loves your adversary. Try to view this person through Jesus' eyes as he walks ahead of you across the bridge to prepare the way. Visualise both parties now crossing the bridge and meeting in the middle. Jesus is standing between you. Is there anything you want to say or do?

> For if you forgive men when they sin against you,
> your heavenly Father will also forgive you.
> But if you do not forgive men their sins, your Father
> will not forgive your sins. (Matthew 6:14,15)

∞ Deep Calls to Deep

Our deepest longing is for intimacy with God. That deep emptiness can only be satisfied by immersing ourselves in the depths of God. God has created us for this divine union. Many people look to others to complete them, to fill that God-shaped hole, but it is only through our relationship with God that we become whole. His nature, or *the divine sperm* as the *Amplified Bible* describes it, is in us, 'for God's nature abides in him [His principle of life, the divine sperm, remains permanently with him]' (1 John 3:9).

Try It for Yourself

Spend some time now reading and reflecting on Psalm 42. Do any thoughts or images spring to mind? Could you write a psalm-like prayer, poem or letter in response?

I have always loved these lines from Psalm 42:

> Deep calls to deep
> in the roar of your waterfalls;
> all your waves and breakers
> have swept over me. (Psalm 42:7)

As I spent time meditating on that wonderful Psalm, I was caught up in its passion and had to write the following response.

Living Water

> Streams of living water
> burst forth with fountains of joy
> and I am soaked –
> soaked in the river
> of your love.[8]

∞ Condemned by Words, Freed by the Word

'You're a failure', 'You're a disappointment', 'You're a jack of all trades and master of none'. These are just some of the negative words spoken over me during my life.

Words are containers of power, and as we internalise these negative words they become like a mantra, 'I'm a failure, I'm a disappointment, I'm jack of all trades and master of none.' In other words, nothing I do is any good!

A friend of mine wonderfully challenged this 'jack of all trades' label that I have been labouring under for years. 'Liz,' she said, 'you're multicreative and multitalented, just like your heavenly Dad, a chip off the old block.' But it takes a lot of positive endorsements to negate one negative comment.

Satan loves to make us feel a failure, because a sense of failure prevents us from achieving our potential in Christ. So we have to challenge that negativity with the power of God's Word. Sometimes the words spoken over us can lead us to feeling shame. But Jesus died wearing a crown of shame so that we could live in freedom and dignity holding our heads high. For God is 'my glory and the lifter of my head' (Psalm 3:3 AMP). I know that I'm not a disappointment to God, because Scripture tells me that he delights in me. 'For the Lord takes delight in his people' (Psalm 149:4).

Have any negative words been spoken over you? Can you bring them to mind now? If so, write them down.

The wonderful thing is that through Scripture we can displace those negative words with God's truth and receive healing for the wounds those words have created. Offer those negative words to God now and ask for his healing.

∞ Positive Thinking God's Way

I have found that the more I reflect on and memorise Scripture, the better able I am to fight my own negative train of thought with positive Scriptural truths. In the desert, Jesus refuted Satan's lies through the power of the Word.

You might want to think about any negative statements and thoughts that frequently flood your mind, and meditate on and memorise the appropriate positive verses of Scripture.

You say	God Says
It's impossible	With me *all* things are possible: 'Jesus replied, "What is impossible with men is possible with God"' (Luke 18:27).
I'm exhausted	Wait on me, I'll renew your strength: 'Those who hope in the Lord will renew their strength' (Isaiah 40:31).
Nobody loves me	I have always loved you: 'I have loved you with an everlasting love' (Jeremiah 31:3).
I can't go on	You can with my help: 'My grace is sufficient for you, for my power is made perfect in weakness' (2 Corinthians 12:9).
I don't know what to do	I'll show you: 'In all your ways know, recognise, and acknowledge Him, and He will direct and make straight and plain your paths' (Proverbs 3:6 AMP).
I can't do it	You can with my help: 'I can do everything through him who gives me strength' (Philippians 4:13).

It's not worth it	It will be – just keep going: 'Let us not become weary in doing good, for at the proper time we will reap a harvest if we do not give up' (Galatians 6:9).
I can't forgive myself	You can, because I have: 'Be kind and compassionate to one another, forgiving each other, just as in Christ God forgave you' (Ephesians 4:32).
I can't make ends meet	I'll supply all your needs: 'And my God will meet all your needs according to his glorious riches in Christ Jesus' (Philippians 4:19).
I'm afraid	I didn't give you a spirit of fear, but of . . . power: 'For God did not give us a spirit of timidity, but a spirit of power, of love and of self-discipline' (2 Timothy 1:7).
I can't handle this	Give it to me and I'll handle it for you: 'Cast your cares on the Lord and he will sustain you' (Psalm 55:22).
I don't have enough faith	I'll give you faith: 'Do not think of yourself more highly than you ought, but rather think of yourself with sober judgement, in accordance with the measure of faith God has given you' (Romans 12:3).
I'm not clever enough	I'll give you wisdom: 'It is because of him that you are in Christ Jesus, who has become for us wisdom from God' (1 Corinthians 1:30).
I'm all alone	I will never leave you on your own: 'Never will I leave you; never will I forsake you' (Hebrews 13:5).[9]

CHAPTER 4

So Let's Get Meditating

❧

Throughout the centuries Christians have discovered many different ways to meditate, some of which I outline in this chapter. I've created a whole variety of meditations throughout this book for you to try by yourself or with others, but I have also included material in this chapter that would be suitable for non-Christians.

As I mentioned in chapter 1, meditation is one of the buzz words of our culture and can be an excellent opportunity for evangelism. I've led meditation sessions at major secular book shops, in public libraries and on radio and mainstream TV. It's possible to reach thousands and possibly even millions of people this way and so is a very exciting mission field.

∞ What If I Meditate and Nothing Happens?

This is perfectly normal. In fact, it is likely to happen quite often.

Don't worry; it's not an achievement test. You've still spent quality time with God and that is real success. Enjoy those 'nothing' moments; when nothing seems to be happening, you are learning how to be with God and enjoy his company, which is at the heart of intimacy. You are also learning how to listen to God rather than bombard him with your anxieties and requests.

Enjoying God's presence, or Sonbathing, as I refer to it, is the essence of contemplation. And if you fall asleep, as many people do, enjoy resting in God's presence. I once led a group where within minutes a guide dog fell asleep and began snoring very loudly. I used this as an illustration of complete relaxation!

∞ Sucking a Sweet Meditation!

In the days of the early monasteries when monks couldn't read, they discovered an innovative way of combining Scripture reading with personal prayer. The *lectio divina* (divine or holy reading) is a form of prayer that has been used for centuries in the church and was popularised by Saint Benedict.

Saint Benedict was born in Italy around 480 and lived a life of prayer as a hermit. He wrote his *Rule* for monks, integrating work and prayer and this *Rule* later became the model for all western monasticism.

The *lectio divina* has been described as the prayer of the listening heart. I like this method of praying the Scriptures because it is quick and simple and is also a great way of taking scriptural gems with you into the rest of the day. This form of meditation can also lead to contemplation, which is the wordless enjoyment of being with God. Its four basic steps are:

- Listen to or **read** aloud a short passage of Scripture several times and see if a word, phrase or image catches your attention. (If it doesn't, then choose one.)

- Stay with that word, phrase or image and ask God what he might be saying to you through it. Continue **reflecting** on this passage absorbing its goodness and allowing it to roll over in your mind (like sucking a sweet).

- Then **respond** in prayer – 'Lord, thank you for . . .'

- Now **rest** – or simply enjoy Sonbathing – in God's presence.

Don't worry if you can't remember all the stages of *lectio divina*. One helpful way of remembering the four steps is the 'Four R's': Read, Reflect, Respond, Rest.

Now, try reading the Psalm below and see how God speaks to you through it. Remember not to analyse it – allow the *eyes of your heart* (Ephesians 1:10) to be opened, and let the Psalm ask questions of you.

> Unless the LORD builds the house,
> its builders labour in vain.
> Unless the LORD watches over the city,
> the watchmen stand guard in vain.
> In vain you rise early
> and stay up late,
> toiling for food to eat –
> for he grants sleep to those he loves. (Psalm 127:1–2)

When I spent some time reflecting on this Psalm recently, I realised that I was still trying to work *for* God rather than *with* him. Writing this book had become such a struggle, and yet what I desperately sought was the ease of God's anointing. I wasn't sleeping; I kept worrying that I would fail, that I wouldn't make the deadline and that the book wouldn't be good enough. I wasn't trusting that God was going to 'build the house'; I was still trying to do it all myself.

The words 'in vain you rise early and stay up late' really spoke to me because I was working such long hours. But as I continued to meditate, the lovely calming words that the Lord 'grants sleep to those he loves' helped me to begin to let go of my worries and begin to trust again. Now when my head hits the pillow and anxieties begin to stir, I repeat to myself, God 'grants sleep to those he loves'.

∞ Walking Meditation

When I lead sessions at large events, I usually have to rush from one venue to another, which creates a state of tension rather than calm. As I'm not naturally a relaxed person, I have to seek God for inner stillness so that I can model calmness rather than stress when leading my workshops!

So I began experimenting with walking and meditating. I would walk at a slower more relaxed pace between venues and tie my breathing into my walking pattern. This created a natural rhythm and an opportunity to practice my breathing exercises at the same time. The overall effect was not only calming but resulted in the unexpected bonus of my being able to share my faith!

As hundreds of conference goers sped along the sea front to their next meeting, I dawdled – contemplatively of course!

The sea-front caretaker stopped me and asked who the crowds of people were. When I explained, he said he wanted to know more about what Christians believe. What an opportunity!

We forget that in our rush to get from *A* to *B* we make ourselves unapproachable. The irony is that some of the workshops people were rushing to were on evangelism!

Stress and busyness tends to lead to shallow breathing from the top part of our lungs, rather than from our diaphragm. This exercise will help you to breathe correctly and can be done anytime, anywhere and is a natural antidote to stress as well as a great reminder to connect with God, the source of all peace and calm.

Try It for Yourself

- Spend a few minutes walking at a slower pace. Feel the calming effect this has upon your body, mind and spirit. Enjoy the natural rhythm of walking at a slower speed.
- Now link your breathing to your walking. Breathe in for two paces, hold your breath for two paces and breathe out for four paces. Repeat this sequence several times.
- Now breathe in for three paces, hold your breath for three paces and breathe out for six paces. Repeat sequence several times.

You can also link Scripture to your rhythmic walking pattern. For example, 'I can do' (three paces breathing in), 'all things through' (three paces holding your breath), 'God who gives me his strength' (six paces breathing out).

You can even experiment with breathing in for four paces, holding your breath for four paces and breathing out for eight paces if you can manage it. See what you find comfortable.

∞ Imaginative Contemplation

St Ignatius of Loyola, the founder of the Jesuits, was born in Spain in 1491. He served as a soldier but was later wounded in battle. During his long convalescence he read *The Life of Christ*, was converted and lived a life of prayer and meditation devising a series of meditations known as his *Spiritual Exercises*.

As part of these exercises, Ignatius developed a simple way to enter into Scripture using the imagination and the senses. Today it would be like producing a movie of a particular Bible passage, often taken from the Gospels, and directing and casting yourself in one of the key roles.

The purpose of engaging with Scripture in this way is so that it comes to life and has more meaning for you. To be in character you would need to research your part by studying Scripture and establishing the context – the what, when, who, why, how, where, and so on. You might begin by asking yourself what the Biblical scene might look like – that is, the setting. Then you would allow the scene to roll in your mind and, in character, engage your senses by imagining what you see, how you interact with others, what you feel, what you hear, what you smell, and so on. This kind of meditation takes practice and is not for everyone, but you may find that it leads to fresh revelations on the character and person of Jesus.

In a group setting recently, I was led in an imaginative contemplation of the Last Supper, and I really struggled to see, hear or feel anything. Other spiritual superstars in the group could even smell the smoke from the oil lamps and the aroma of fresh bread. I got nothing.

I think the reason for this, apart from tiredness, was that I needed to read the passage of Scripture myself before I could engage with it in an imaginative way.

An alternative way on this occasion was for me to watch a video of the *Gospel of Matthew*. As I viewed this particular scene, Scripture came to life, and I was deeply moved. Some of the hard work had been done for me, and I could now literally pause the video and return to this scene in my imagination. I imagined that I was one of the disciples and I chatted to Jesus asking him a series of questions. He was so affirming of me and seemed to say, 'I love you just as much as each one of these disciples of mine. Can you receive the abundance of my love for you?' Now that was a challenge, because I struggle in this area. So, as part of my ongoing journey into God, I knew I needed to spend more time allowing myself to be loved by God.

Here is a contemporary exploration of the Prodigal Son which you might like to try.

A Contemporary Exploration of the Prodigal

Read Luke 15, verses 11–32, and imagine yourself stepping into the shoes of a rebellious son or daughter as this scene is now transposed into the twenty-first century.

- How does it feel to be you? What are you wearing? What are you thinking?

- How do you feel about your father? What does he look like? How old is he? Is he gentle or stern? What is he wearing? How does he speak?

- What does your older brother look like? How much older is he than you? Is he your father's favourite or are you? How do you feel about him?

- Now imagine yourself saying to your father, 'I want my share of your money, and I want it now.' How do you feel – happy, angry? What do you think your father is thinking and feeling?

- Imagine yourself turning your back on your family now for ever. How does that feel? Is it painful or a relief to say goodbye?

- Visualise yourself entering Hollywood (or any other place you've always dreamed of going). This is the land of hopes and dreams where the rich and famous live, work and party . . . What does Hollywood look like? What sounds or music can you hear?

- Money and power speak in Hollywood, so who are your new friends now? Where do they 'hang out'? Which celebrities do you imagine seeing? What do they do all day and all night? What do you do? Do you think your new friends like you or your money?

- Now enjoy the excitement of being free at last, free to live the excesses of the celebrity lifestyle you've always dreamed of. A friend to the stars attending countless Hollywood premiers and parties. Free to do exactly what you want, when you want to – to live life to the full – wildly, selfishly and extravagantly.

- Your money has now run out . . . What does it feel like to be with the rich and famous and not even have enough money to buy a round of drinks? Where are your friends now? How do they treat you? Who cares about you? How does it feel seeing humiliating pictures of yourself splashed across the front pages of the tabloid newspapers saying, 'Down, and Out. Forget this A-List Loser'? How does it feel to be despised and totally alone – to be irrelevant ... to be ignored? Feel the pain of that loneliness now ... How does it feel to be starving ... dirty ... humiliated ... to be reduced to rummaging through Hollywood bins for food, begging for money and sleeping rough on the streets you once rode in a limousine?

- Now imagine turning your back on this lifestyle that promised so much but delivered so little. How does it feel to know that you've failed, to feel defeated, empty and worthless ... to be totally desperate? Now think about your home again ... Even your father's employees are treated better than this. Do you think your father might take you back if you worked as one of his labourers?

- Now imagine the long, exhausting journey home ...

- Are you worried about seeing your father again? What are you going to say to him if he is willing to see you?

- Now catch sight of your father in the distance ... He is running towards you ... with his arms outstretched. This is more than you could have hoped for, more than you deserve. You're lost for words as you feel the warmth and tenderness of his embrace. How are you feeling now? Hear yourself saying,

'Father, I've really messed up. I don't even deserve to be called your son any more.' But your father is so overjoyed that he's already organising a lavish party in your honour.

- Your brother, meanwhile, is angry and jealous at the way you're being treated considering how you've behaved, and he's planning to boycott the party. How do you feel about your brother now?

- Your father pleads with him, 'Son, you're always here with me, and what's mine is yours. But we have to celebrate because I thought your brother was dead, but now he's here and he's alive.'

- See your father presenting you with designer clothes and footwear . . . and placing the family ring on your finger. Visualise the rich colourful spread of food in front of you . . . the music . . . the dancing . . . the champagne . . . the laughter . . . all your friends and family gathered round celebrating your return.

- Spend some time now enjoying the atmosphere and extravagance of a *real* party, where love is the motivation not money, and where you matter because you mean *everything* to your father.

- You've truly *come home*. . .

Even Jesus Took His Time!

Jesus wasn't exactly in a rush to heal Lazarus. He took his time. In fact, he waited several days before going to his friend's house.

Here is another exercise in imaginative contemplation. As you read this passage from John's Gospel, allow it to play on the video screen of your mind. You can pause it at any point and rewind or even fast forward. Imagine that you are one of the sisters in this story. How are you feeling? What can you see and smell? What might you want to say to Jesus at the beginning of this passage? When Lazarus dies, what's your response? What's your reaction to Jesus' tears? What's Jesus saying to you now? When Lazarus rises from the dead, what's your reaction?

> Now a man named Lazarus was sick. He was from Bethany, the village of Mary and her sister Martha. This Mary, whose brother Lazarus now lay sick, was the same one who poured perfume on the Lord and wiped his feet with her hair. So the sisters sent word to Jesus, 'Lord, the one you love is sick.'
>
> When he heard this, Jesus said, 'This sickness will not end in death. No, it is for God's glory so that God's Son may be glorified through it.' Jesus loved Martha and her sister and Lazarus. Yet when he heard that Lazarus was sick, he stayed where he was two more days . . . When Martha heard that Jesus was coming, she went out to meet him, but Mary stayed at home. . . .
>
> When Mary reached the place where Jesus was and saw him, she fell at his feet and said, 'Lord, if you had been here, my brother would not have died.'
>
> When Jesus saw her weeping, and the Jews who had come along with her also weeping, he was deeply moved in spirit and troubled. 'Where have you laid him?' he asked.
>
> 'Come and see, Lord,' they replied.
>
> Jesus wept.
>
> Then the Jews said, 'See how he loved him!'
>
> But some of them said, 'Could not he who opened the eyes of the blind man have kept this man from dying?'

Jesus, once more deeply moved, came to the tomb . . . 'Take away the stone,' he said.

'But, Lord,' said Martha, the sister of the dead man, 'by this time there is a bad odour, for he has been there four days.'

Then Jesus said, 'Did I not tell you that if you believed, you would see the glory of God?' . . . When he had said this, Jesus called in a loud voice, 'Lazarus, come out!' The dead man came out, his hands and feet wrapped with strips of linen, and a cloth around his face. (John 11:1–6, 20, 32–40, 43, 44)

God sometimes keeps us waiting such a long time before he answers our prayers, that we assume he hasn't heard them or doesn't want to answer them. Like Mary and Martha, however, we have to wait because he is working out his greater purposes in our lives. Can you think of examples when God has kept you waiting?

God's Love Will Always Pursue You

'God's love is irresistible,' says a friend of mine, 'whenever I sin and go away from God, it's always his love that draws me back.' No matter what we've done, whether we know God or not, or whether we're too busy even to notice him, God's love will always pursue us. He will leave the ninety-nine sheep to seek out the lost one; such is the faithfulness of his love for us.

Here's yet another exercise in spiritual, imaginative contemplation. The story of the lost sheep is a wonderful picture of God's love. It can also be used as a prayer for family and friends that don't know God, or who have turned away from him. It is a timely reminder that when we make mistakes and get caught up in the barbed wire of life, God will always come looking for us.

Spend some time now reflecting on this story that Jesus told. Do any thoughts or images spring to mind?

> If any of you has a hundred sheep, and one of them gets lost, what will you do? Won't you leave the ninety-nine in the field and go and look for the lost sheep until you find it? And when you find it, you will be so glad that you will put it on your shoulder and carry it home. Then you will call in your friends and neighbours and say, 'Let's celebrate! I've found my lost sheep.'
>
> Jesus said, 'In the same way there is more happiness in heaven because of one sinner who turns to God than over ninety-nine good people who don't need to.' (Luke 15:4–7 CEV)

∞ And If You Can't Sleep

> I'm awake all night – not a wink of sleep; I can't even say what's bothering me. (Psalm 77:4 MSG)

I have a prayer card that says, 'There's little point counting sheep when you can talk to the Shepherd!'

As my sleep tends to be interrupted these days, I have begun to develop a whole series of strategies to cope with this. I generally see it positively as an opportunity to spend time with God – a ready-made prayer time.

I try to focus on God, rather than on my own anxieties, which always loom larger than life in the early hours of the morning. I find praying the Jesus Prayer particularly helpful, as it calms my mind and helps me to focus on Jesus – the solution to my problem. I've also developed a way of reflecting on and memorising Scripture. I call it Alphabet Scripture and find it much more edifying than counting sheep. I go through each letter of the alphabet and allow it to trigger a Scripture in my mind working through from A to Z. This way, I'm feeding myself even in the middle of the night and mercifully I'm often asleep before I reach Z!

Alphabet Scripture

- **A**bide in me and I will abide in you. (John 15:4)
- **B**e transformed by the renewing of your mind. (Romans 12:2)
- **C**ast your cares on the Lord and he will sustain you. (Psalm 55:22)
- **D**eep calls to deep . . . (Psalm 42:7)
- **E**ven youths grow tired and weary but those who hope in the Lord will renew their strength. (Isaiah 40:31)
- **F**ix your eyes on things above. (Hebrews 12:2)
- **G**od is faithful and he will do it. (1 Thessalonians 5:24)
- **H**e will keep in perfect peace those who will put their trust in him. (Isaiah 26:3)
- **I**n quietness and trust is your strength. (Isaiah 30:15)
- **J**udge not lest you be judged. (Matthew 7:1)
- **K**eep my commandments. (Exodus 20:6)
- **L**ove the Lord your God with all your heart. (Proverbs 3:5)
- **M**y grace is sufficient for you, for my power is made perfect in weakness. (2 Corinthians 12:9)

- Nothing can separate us from the love of God. (Romans 8:38–9)
- O Israel put your hope in the Lord. (Psalm 130:7)
- Praise the Lord, O my soul, and forget not all his benefits. (Psalm 103:2)
- Quench not the Spirit's fire. (1 Thessalonians 5:19)
- Resist the devil, and he will flee. (James 4:7)
- Surely goodness and mercy will follow me all the days of my life. (Psalm 23:6)
- Take every thought captive and make it obedient to Christ. (2 Corinthians 10:5)
- Underneath are the everlasting arms. (Deuteronomy 33:27)
- Vengeance is mine says the Lord. (Hebrews 10:30)
- Without faith it is impossible to please God. (Hebrews 11:6)
- Your life is now hidden with Christ in God. (Colossians 3:3)
- . . . Zion's sake I will not keep silent. (Isaiah 62:1)

Sometimes, God has woken me up to pray for somebody in the early hours of the morning. On one particular occasion it was a friend who was contemplating suicide. I didn't know this at the time, but felt prompted to pray and to get in touch with her as soon as possible. My friend found this to be such a source of encouragement that it helped turn her circumstances around. The peak time for committing suicide is in the early hours of the morning, so it is a very important time to pray and intercede for others.

∞ Practicing the Presence of God

I love the idea that God is with me throughout my day, so everything I do can become a form of prayer. This is called 'practicing the presence of God'. Back in the seventeenth century, Brother Lawrence, a busy monk in a French monastery wrote a little book called *The Practice of the Presence of God*. He saw his work in the kitchen as an extension of his more formal times of prayer shared with the other monks. In the chaos and busyness of the twenty-first century, this seventeenth century monk has much to say to us: 'The time of business does not differ with me from the time of prayer; and in the noise and clatter of my kitchen, while several persons are at the same time calling for different things, I possess God in as great tranquillity as if I were upon my knees.'[10]

Brother Lawrence also suggested praying short simple prayers throughout the day. Keeping things simple is at the heart of prayer. If God tells us to come to him as *little children* (Matthew 19:14), then our prayers don't have to be complex or rambling.

The average text message is very short, but it communicates a message. How about trying to increase your awareness of God throughout your day. You could even send him a short text like 'I luv U'. It could transform your prayer life.

Sometimes when I try to practice the presence of God, I spend most of my day thinking about something or someone else. Often I allow worry to take centre stage. If I were to pray as much as I worry, I would be mightily blessed! Sometimes anger fuels my day and I visualise the person and rehearse angry conversations in my mind. At other times, someone I admire, or a friend who has said something encouraging, fills my thoughts for that day. It's so easy to practice the presence of others; their faces are saved on the screen savers of my mind and pop up at regular intervals throughout the day. The reassuring thing is that if you can practice the presence of someone else, then you can certainly practice the presence of God. Ask God to be your screen saver. In fact, you could ask God to help you to use your worries, fears, or preoccupations as a trigger to focus on him. Try praying this prayer, 'Lord, may my thoughts turn towards you as often as they do towards [fill in the name of the person].'

∞ Mary – a Natural Contemplative

Mary, the mother of Jesus, carried the Word of God inside her. She was a natural contemplative, who 'treasured' God's words to her and 'pondered them in her heart' (Luke 2:19). Her full attention was focused on God and what he was calling her to do. We have much to learn from Mary whose humble obedience and attentiveness to God changed the course of history.

Spend some time now reflecting on Mary's song:

My soul glorifies the Lord
    and my spirit rejoices in God my Saviour,
for he has been mindful
    of the humble state of his servant.
From now on all generations will call me blessed,
    for the Mighty One has done great things for me –
    holy is his name. (Luke 1:46–49)

What *great things* has God done in your life? You might want to list them in a journal or notebook. Now spend some time thanking God for his faithfulness.

∞ Exploring Silence

To find the pathway that leads to intimacy with God, we need to discover the gift of silence. Silence is the language of lovers enabling us to draw closer to the Father heart of God. In silence it is easier to hear God, as noise can be like a spiritual pollution drowning out his voice. Try having an important conversation with a loved one on a mobile whilst travelling on a bus or train! The noise and confusion of voices makes it very difficult to hear, let alone to speak. Our times of silence can be a real investment, providing wells of living water that we can draw from.

Try It for Yourself

Spend one minute now in silence. Notice the thoughts that crowd into your mind. Keep giving these thoughts to God, so that you can focus on him. Spend a further minute Sonbathing – just relaxing and enjoying his company. In time, as you get used to silence, you will begin to enjoy it and be able to spend longer in God's company in this way.

∞ Receiving God's Love

Psalm 139 is a wonderful expression of God's love for us. Not everyone finds this psalm comfortable reading, however, especially if they have had difficult childhood experiences. Applying the words of Psalm 139 to my own life has been a painful but healing journey.

One way of meditating on this psalm is to focus on just one or two lines of the psalm at a time, then pause and reflect. I have made some suggestions of how you might do this. Be aware of the words or phrases which affect you either positively or negatively. What is God saying to you through these words or phrases? God's Word has the power to heal, so be open to receive his healing as you read.

> For you created my inmost being;
> you knit me together in my
> mother's womb.
> I praise you because I am fearfully
> and wonderfully made;
> your works are wonderful,
> I know that full well.
> My frame was not hidden from you
> when I was made in the secret place.
> When I was woven together in the
> depths of the earth,
> your eyes saw my unformed body.
> All the days ordained for me
> were written in your book
> before one of them came to be.
> How precious to me are your
> thoughts, O God!
> How vast is the sum of them!
> Were I to count them,
> they would outnumber the grains of sand.
> When I awake,
> I am still with you. (vv. 13–18)

You might like to write your own personal response to Psalm 139 like I've done below. I found this a very healing process:

> Thank you, Lord,
> for the cutting and weaving
> for that first umbilical knot
> you were shaping
> and forming
> all that I was to become
>
> Thank you, Lord,
> for the ups and downs
> the unders and the overs
> you were weaving
> beauty and purpose
> into my life.[11]

One of the most helpful things that I have ever been encouraged to do is to explore the different ways God has shown his love for me. It is so easy to be negative and to focus on all that is going wrong in life, but this tends to obscure God. But becoming more aware of God's loving footprints across my life has been a life changing experience. You might like to try this yourself.

- Write down all the different ways God has shown his love for you in the past 24 hours. (It could be through friends, a smile, a telephone conversation, a card, an email etc)

- Write down all the different ways God has shown his love for you in the past year.

- Write down all the different ways God has shown his love for you in the past five years.

- Finally, write down all the different ways God has shown his love for you since you were born. (You might find it helpful to refer to the exercise on page 41 where you charted God's presence in your life's journey.)

Now Sonbathe in God's presence and receive his unconditional love for you.

A Special Love Note from God to You

You're valuable
You're special
You're beautiful
You're precious
You're lovable
You're unique
You're mine
And I LOVE YOU xoxoxo

∞ The Power of Humility

I meet quite a few famous Christians in the work that I do, but what really impresses me is not a person's apparent success, but their radical humility. This has really challenged me and made me aware of my own lack of humility.

During this period of burnout, I feel as though I have been broken down from a clay pot of my own design, to a formless blob of clay. A painful process, but at least a lump of clay is malleable and can be remoulded by the Master Potter. 'Like clay in the hand of the potter, so are you in my hand' (Jeremiah 18:6). But essentially true humility is brokenness.

As you read this passage from Jeremiah, think about the ways you have created your own clay pot. What shape is it? What colour is it? Are you proud of it? Does it have your name on? Ask God what he thinks about your pot?

> This is the word that came to Jeremiah from the LORD: 'Go down to the potter's house, and there I will give you my message.' So I went down to the potter's house, and I saw him working at the wheel. But the pot he was shaping from the clay was marred in his hands; so the potter formed it into another pot, shaping it as it seemed best to him. (Jeremiah 18:1–4)

I am an impatient activist so I tend to wear myself out trying to make things happen rather than waiting and trusting in God's timing. My experience of burnout has really highlighted the fact that God uses my fragility and weakness rather than my strength. Paul learned humility through his 'thorn in the flesh' (2 Corinthians 12:7), and the acceptance of that weakness caused radical transformation in his life and the lives of countless others. It is when the alabaster jug of pride is broken, that the oil of God's anointing can be fully released. Consider this passage from Mark:

> While he was in Bethany, reclining at the table in the home of a man known as Simon the Leper, a woman came with an alabaster jar of very expensive perfume, made of pure nard. She broke the jar and poured the perfume on his head. Some of those present were saying indignantly to one another,

'Why waste this perfume? It could have been sold for more than a year's wages and the money given to the poor.' And they rebuked her harshly. 'Leave her alone,' said Jesus. 'Why are you bothering her? She has done a beautiful thing to me.' (Mark 14:3–6)

While everyone seems to be locked into the relentless chase for money, success and fame, try asking God to help you to develop the kind of radical humility that Jesus modelled, that is so beautifully expressed in the Beatitudes. It's a wonderful antidote to our celebrity culture. The following verses express the kind of humility that Christ himself had.

> Christ was truly God.
> But he did not try to remain
>   equal with God.
> Instead he gave up everything
>   and became a slave,
> when he became
>   like one of us.
> Christ was humble.
> He obeyed God and even died
>   on a cross.
> Then God gave Christ
>   the highest place
> and honoured his name
>   above all others.
>   (Philippians 2:6–9 CEV)

Ask yourself: How weak am I prepared to be? Then try meditating on a different beatitude each day asking God to speak to you through it.

Blessed are the poor in spirit, for theirs is the kingdom of
heaven.

Blessed are those who mourn, for they will be comforted.

Blessed are the meek, for they will inherit the earth.

Blessed are those who hunger and thirst for righteousness,
for they will be filled.

Blessed are the merciful, for they will be shown mercy.

Blessed are the pure in heart, for they will see God.

Blessed are the peacemakers, for they will be called sons
of God.

Blessed are those who are persecuted because of righteousness,
for theirs is the kingdom of heaven.

(Matthew 5:3–10)

∾ The Armour of God

The enemy will do his utmost to prevent us from becoming more intimate with God. He'd rather we were all too busy and worn out to explore new pathways of drawing closer to God.

For instance, I have had to dictate most of this book using voice software because RSI (repetitive strain injury) has prevented me from typing. There seems to have been a lot of opposition to me writing this book. The enemy has sought to undermine me and destroy my peace in any way he could.

But the enemy is also very predictable. Whenever I undertake anything of great spiritual significance, he attacks my health, which has the effect of unsettling me both emotionally and spiritually. But the enemy is a defeated liar and God has more than met my needs during this period, even providing me with extra intercessory prayer back up to help me complete this book. It feels like I'm being supported by God's special cavalry.

My experience of burnout has also opened up new creative pathways for me to encounter God, because I've had the luxury of time off in the middle of writing this book. I needed to become sufficiently weak for God's strength and power to flow through me. I'm sure the enemy would much rather that I was now burning myself out *for* God than spend so much time *with* God, because the enemy loves to drive us so that we are no longer effective. In fact, we are told in Daniel that one of the enemy's tactics is to 'wear out the saints' (Daniel 7:25 AMP).

The various arm supports that I have also needed to wear to be able to edit this book have reminded me of the armour of God, mentioned in Ephesians 6. As I begin work, I visualise putting on God's breastplate of integrity, his shoes of peace, his helmet of salvation, his belt of truth, and I take up my shield of faith, knowing that nothing is going to stop me from fulfilling the call of God on my life to complete this book! Finally, I take up the sword of the Spirit which is the Word of God – knowing that this is my ultimate weapon against the enemy's tactics.

Are you facing a difficult challenge? Do you need to put on God's armour today? A friend of mine prays this Scripture daily, and as she does so, she reminds herself that she is clothing herself in the wonderful garments of God's presence.

Spend some time now meditating on each line of this Scripture and see if any particular words or phrases become highlighted for you or seem to speak personally about your circumstances. What might God be saying to you?

Therefore put on God's complete armour, that you may be able to resist and stand your ground on the evil day [of danger], and, having done all [the crisis demands], to stand [firmly in your place].

Stand therefore [hold your ground], having tightened the belt of truth around your loins and having put on the breast-plate of integrity and of moral rectitude and right standing with God.

And having shod your feet in preparation [to face the enemy with the firm-footed stability, the promptness, and the readiness produced by the good news] of the Gospel of peace.

Lift up over all the [covering] shield of saving faith, upon which you can quench all the flaming missiles of the wicked [one].

And take the helmet of salvation and the sword that the Spirit wields, which is the Word of God.

(Ephesians 6:13–17 AMP)

∞ Reviewing the Year

People automatically associate the New Year with New Year resolutions, which are often broken very quickly. The favourite resolution seems to be either losing weight or getting fitter. On New Year's Eve, there is always an endless stream of TV programmes reviewing the year, so I decided to do my own highs and lows of 2003.

I divided a page of my journal into two columns with the headings *highs* and *lows*. As 2003 had not been a particularly good year, I thought that all the problems I had encountered would dominate and very few highs would emerge. The reverse was true. The list of highs was three times longer than the list of lows, and many of the lows had given rise to unexpected blessings!

Although many of the problems that had caused the lows of 2003 were still an issue, they had now retreated into the background, because God had brought about an amazing transformation in me. I'd regained my sense of humour, and I'd begun to let go of work as an idol. I began to invite people to my house again for meals. Friends and children came to stay and even neighbours popped in. Before, I used to keep the curtains firmly closed shutting everyone out so that I could work. An imaginary sign was firmly fixed on my door saying, 'Evangelist at Work – Keep Out!'

Now that I was learning how to let God lead me, rather than strive, new and exciting opportunities were emerging on the horizon of 2004 and 2005. What seemed like such failure, in not achieving the original deadline for this book, was no longer an issue. God's timing is always perfect, even when he seems to be late. As I prayerfully continued to evaluate my highs and lows, the two columns seemed to merge and become the highlights of 2003. I was then able to thank God for all he had done in my life, because I was now seeing the year through his eyes rather than my own. What a difference in perspective!

Review your past year's listing of highs and lows. Don't think about this too much. Simply write down the first things that spring immediately to mind. Is there any connection between the two columns? Where can you see evidence of God's transforming power at work?

Now ask God what his desire is for you in the year ahead?

When I asked God these questions, I sensed that God's reply was, 'Come to me, come with me, be with me . . . relax . . . I want you to enjoy your life.'

This was rather a shock, as there was nothing about all the work God wanted me to do for him. Instead, I sensed that I needed to surrender all that I am and all that I have to him and let him take care of the rest.

Although our shopping list of needs and desires in the coming year might be very long, God's list is very short. His desire is for us to know him more and to enter into a deeper and more intimate relationship with him. His message is simple, 'Know my love, receive my love, respond to my love.'

∞ Learning How to Relax

Many people tell me they don't know how to relax, so here are some techniques to help you.

Five Quick Ways to Relax Your Body

1. **Tension check** – Scan your body from head to toe and when you become aware of an area of tension or discomfort, gently tense it and release it and then relax.

2. **Shower relaxation** – Imagine taking a warm shower or bath and allow the water to soothe away any discomfort or distress so that you feel relaxed and refreshed.

3. **Massage** – Gently massage your forehead, head and neck as though you were shampooing your hair. You'll find it wonderfully relaxing.

4. **Word response** – Choose a word or brief phrase that helps you to relax such as *peace, relax, be still,* and so on. Close your eyes and slowly repeat this word or phrase to yourself until you start to experience its meaning.

5. **Peaceful place** – Imagine a beautiful place, perhaps a forest, park, country lane or sandy beach. Use all your senses to experience this place fully. What does it look like? What can you hear? What can you feel and smell?

Tuning In to Your Body (Five Minutes)

1. Lie on your back or sit comfortably and close your eyes.

2. Become aware of your body as a whole including the places where it contacts the floor, bed or chair.

3. Focus on the toes of your right foot. Can you feel any sensations? As you breathe, imagine your breath flowing down your body and out through your toes. Now do the same focusing on your left foot.

4. Gradually move up the body from your toes, to the soles of your feet and to your ankles – becoming aware of any sensations and feeling your breath flowing into your feet.

5. Now feel your breath flowing into your right leg ...
your left leg ... your right knee ... your left knee ...
your right hip ... your left hip ... your pelvis ...
your lower abdomen ... your lower back ... your
upper back ... your chest ... your shoulders ... your
fingers ... your hands ... your right arm ... your left
arm ... your neck and throat ... your chin ... your
face ... the back of your head ... the top of your
head.

6. Rest and enjoy the relaxation for several minutes,
and then gradually open your eyes, have a stretch
and then move into the rest of your day.

Healing Relaxation (Five Minutes)

1. Make yourself comfortable and then close your eyes.

2. Now become aware of your body and check out how
it feels. Do parts of your body feel tense and tired? If
so, identify these areas.

3. Become aware of your breathing, and each time you
breathe in, imagine the Holy Spirit flowing through
you, energising each cell in your body. Then as you
exhale, imagine any tension, tiredness, pain or
discomfort flowing out through your body.

4. Now visualise yourself lying on a warm beach with
the sun streaming down on your body. Relax and
enjoy sinking into the warm sand beneath you.

5. Focus on your breathing again and as you inhale
imagine that you are breathing in God's love.

6. Finally, simply Sonbathe – relaxing and enjoying God's presence.

Deep Relaxation (Fifteen Minutes)

1. Find somewhere comfortable to lie down. Lie with your arms resting by your sides and your legs slightly apart.

2. Become aware of your whole body and the places where it touches the floor or bed.

3. Close your eyes and focus your attention on your feet. You might want to wiggle your toes and flex your feet, and then let go of any tension. Feel them sinking into the floor.

4. Now become aware of your lower legs, your thighs and your hips. Feel them becoming heavier and heavier as they sink into the floor.

5. Breathe in deeply and breathe out slowly several times . . . Feel your breath flowing from your chest cavity down into your abdomen.

6. Now become aware of your neck and throat softening . . . and repeat the word *relax* . . . to yourself several times as you continue to breathe in deeply and out slowly.

7. Feel your shoulders, arms and hands becoming heavier as they sink into the floor.

8. Feel any tension in your face and head melting away.

9. Check that your whole body is completely relaxed, as you continue to breathe in deeply and breathe out slowly. If you find any areas of discomfort just imagine that part of your body sinking into the floor. Say to yourself, 'I am relaxed . . . I am completely relaxed.'

10. Continue enjoying resting and relaxing for several minutes. Then, gradually open your eyes, wiggle your toes and have a stretch. When you are ready sit up.

∞ Meditations for Everyday Life

Rushing to work? Children making demands? Tuning into God can be a real struggle, but God's blessings are new every morning.

Kick-Starting Your Day with God

Our natural inclination when we start the day is to forget God and follow our own agenda. But a bad start to the day will colour the rest of it. God wants us to come to him because we love him, rather than out of a sense of duty.

Just as you might naturally talk to your husband or wife first thing in the morning, try to spend some time with God committing your day to him. You could meditate in the shower, if this is the only time you have on your own. Breathe in the presence of Jesus taking several deep breaths, and then bring a Scripture to mind.

As you dash off to work imagine he's in the passenger seat and chat to him about your day. You could listen to a Scripture tape as you drive to work or enjoy a praise and worship CD. Jesus talked to his father while he was out on the hills, so try talking to yours as you drive to work, go to the shops or take the kids to school. As you maximise your awareness of God by starting every day with him, you'll be amazed at the difference it makes to the rest of your day.

Here are some Scriptures to get you started:

- I can do everything with the help of Christ (Philippians 4:13 NLT).

- Above all, love each other deeply, because love covers over a multitude of sins (1 Peter 4:8).

- Under pressure, your faith-life is forced into the open and shows its true colours (James 1:3 MSG).

- We don't know why things happen as they do, but we don't give up (2 Corinthians 4:8 LB).

- He gives power to those who are tired and worn out; he offers strength to the weak (Isaiah 40:29 NLT).

- So let's keep focused on that goal, those of us who want everything God has for us (Philippians 3:15 MSG).

- A cheerful disposition is good for your health; gloom and doom leave you bone-tired (Proverbs 17:22 MSG).

- I'm doing the very best I can, and I'm doing it at home, where it counts (Psalm 101:2 MSG).

- I will lift up mine eyes to the hills – where does my help come from? My help comes from the LORD (Psalm 121:1–2).

- Because of the LORD's great love we are not consumed, for his compassions never fail. They are new every morning; great is your faithfulness (Lamentations 3:22–23).

Prayer

Lord, help me to make you my priority – the centre of everything I say, think and do today. Help me to respect my body and to use my energy wisely. Show me those things you are calling me to do and those things I need to say 'no' to. Help me to trust in your timing, to be led by you and not driven by my own desires and ambitions. Help me to hear and be obedient to your 'still small voice' whispering into every corner of my life.

Travelling to and from Work

Even a busy journey to and from work, slowed down by traffic jams or delayed trains or buses, can be an opportunity to reflect on Scripture. While other people may be taking their road rage into the workplace or their homes, Christians have an alternative. If we really believe and seize upon the help available to us through Scripture then we will be able to stay calm.

Jesus rebuked the wind and spoke to the waves, '"Quiet! Be still!" Then the wind died down and it was completely calm' (Mark 4:39).

As we reflect on Scripture we have spiritual truth at our fingertips, ready to use at our disposal. We can wield the mighty sword of the Spirit – God's Word in any and every situation. If we included Scripture in all our daily communications with friends, our conversations would be far more edifying.

Ask your friends to text or email you Scripture and don't forget to do the same for them. That way you'll have a ready stock of Scriptures to draw upon.

During Work

Even though your day might be impossibly busy or challenging, take time to listen to the 'gentle whisper' (1 Kings 19:12) of God's Holy Spirit. Those inner promptings can tell you when to stop and take time out. 'You chart the path ahead of me, and tell me where to stop and rest' (Psalm 139:3 LB).

If you can, go for a walk and consciously try to switch off from work. Many people feel closer to God when they go for a walk and it can be a real source of relaxation and inspiration, even in a built-up city. Some people find that the fresh air clears their heads and even helps them to generate new ideas.

But if you only get moments to pause throughout the day, seize these moments positively. Consciously switch off from work and into God, like plugging your mobile in to an electricity source to recharge it. Be creative with your time and have a supply of Scripture one liners to hand and talk to God each time you have a coffee break or visit the bathroom etc.

Time Out with God Visiting the Gym!

My time at the gym is important not just recreationally but because it has become an extension of my prayer time. I am lost in a world of my own, enjoying God's company and reflecting on Scripture. In fact, I am often disappointed if I bump into someone I know because it really changes the dynamics of me spending quality time with God. Suddenly I find myself caught up in the clutter of conversation, the 'how am I's' and 'how are you's', which can be such meaningless transactions.

I often pray the Jesus Prayer (see chapter 3) while I'm on the treadmill walking or jogging, when I'm doing abdominal crunches, stretching or even swimming.

I love the sauna because it helps me to relax and unwind. The glass sand timer on the wall is also a wonderful visual aid to prayer. It is graduated in five-, ten- and fifteen-minute segments and so I sometimes meditate for a specific period of time as I watch the sand trickle through. Although I'm usually lying down wrapped in a towel, it reminds me of my nakedness and vulnerability before God. When others join me in the sauna, I focus my prayers on them asking God to bless them.

As I shower in cold water afterwards, I'm reminded of the refreshment that is available to me every time I remember to connect with God. Water also reminds me of the importance of the Holy Spirit in my life and my need to be filled daily.

Ten Popular Relaxation and Meditation Techniques

1. Repeating a meaningful word or phrase like Jesus, Abba, Emmanuel etc.

2. Focusing on your breathing.

3. Becoming aware of the tensions in your body and then releasing them.

4. Focusing on a simple visual object.

5. Imagining a peaceful place.

6. Reflecting on the Bible or other sacred writings.

7. Gazing at sacred art, such as Rembrandt's *The Prodigal*, or icons and so on.

8. Contemplating the beauty in nature.

9. Prayer walking.

10. Listening to music.

The One-Minute Meditation

Be still, and know that I am God. (Psalm 46:10)

Spend approximately fifteen seconds focusing on your breathing, breathing in and out deeply and slowly.

Now repeat the following Scripture to yourself. You might like to emphasise a different word each time you repeat it, such as:

Be *still* and know that I am God
Be still and *know* that I am God
Be still and know that *I* am God
Be still and know that I am *God*

Now continue to repeat just the words *be still ... be still ... be still* to yourself on each out breath ... until the end of the minute.

The One-Word Meditation (Two Minutes of Calm)

> But the fruit of the Spirit is love, joy, peace, patience, kindness, goodness, faithfulness, gentleness and self-control. (Galatians 5:22–23)

To calm your mind and to focus your attention on God try this simple meditation:

Sit quietly in a room where you can feel relaxed and focus on *one* aspect of the fruit of the Spirit. Choose from:

- Love
- Joy
- Peace
- Patience
- Kindness
- Goodness
- Faithfulness
- Gentleness
- Self-control

See this word passing across your mind like a screen saver (on your computer) and focus on this quality for a few minutes.

You may want to finish your meditation by asking God to develop that quality more fully in your life.

Try to focus on a different aspect of the fruit of the Spirit each week – it's likely to be character changing, if not life changing!

Palms Up, Palms Down (Five-Minute Stress Buster)

Sitting or lying down in a comfortable position with the palms of your hands facing upwards, become aware of your breathing deepening and slowing. (One minute.)

Now turning the palms of your hands over to face the floor, release to God all the things that are troubling you at the moment. You might want to imagine yourself removing a heavy back pack from your shoulders, and unpacking all the rocks and stones that have been weighing you down . . . Give to God all those people, situations and circumstances that have been worrying you. (Two minutes.)

> Cast your burden on the Lord [releasing the full weight of it] and He will sustain you. (Psalm 55:22 AMP)

Now, turning the palms of your hands upwards again, spend a few minutes receiving God's love . . . his joy . . . and his peace. (Two minutes.)[12]

Savouring the Lord's Prayer

A really relaxing and more meaningful way to read the Lord's Prayer is to combine it with your breathing. As you inhale, try saying the first line of the prayer to yourself and then exhale. On the second inhalation, say the second line of the Lord's Prayer and then exhale. Continue this pattern of breathing until you have read the whole prayer.

[inhale]	My Father in heaven	[exhale]
[inhale]	your name is Holy	[exhale]
[inhale]	May your kingdom come	[exhale]
[inhale]	and your will be done	[exhale]
[inhale]	on earth as it is in heaven	[exhale]
[inhale]	Give me all I need for today	[exhale]
[inhale]	And forgive me my sins	[exhale]
[inhale]	as I forgive others theirs.	[exhale]
[inhale]	Don't allow me to be tempted	[exhale]
[inhale]	and deliver me from evil	[exhale]
[inhale]	Amen	[exhale]

Five Minutes of Peace

Gradually become aware of your breathing.

Continue being aware of the flow of your breath as you quietly repeat to yourself . . . 'my body is relaxed . . . my heartbeat is steady . . . my mind is calm and peaceful . . . my heart is open to God . . . with every breath I am more deeply at peace . . .'

Now as you breathe, become aware of that peace deepening within you . . .

Now imagine Jesus saying to you, 'My peace I give you . . . Do not let your hearts be troubled and do not be afraid' (John 14:27). Drink in that peace now . . .

You might want to reply, 'Yes Lord, I receive the gift of your peace and I receive it now into my body, my mind and my spirit . . .'

And finally, thank God for his precious gift of peace as you gradually open your eyes, and become aware of your surroundings again.

You R What U Think!

For as he thinks in his heart, so is he. (Proverbs 23:7 AMP)

Try taking an inventory of your thoughts:

- What have you been thinking about in the past few minutes?
- How do those thoughts make you feel?

Our thoughts, as well as our words, are containers of power – either creative or destructive. What we think and say is an indication of what is really in our hearts.

If you feel caught up in a cycle of negative thinking, surrender this to God and ask for his forgiveness. Also ask him to give you the strength to change. If you are critical of yourself or others try praying this prayer:

Lord, please help me to stop thinking negatively about . . . Help me to see the love you have for . . . , so I can see . . . through your eyes.

Developing an Attitude of Gratitude (Five Minutes)

1. Spend a few minutes reviewing all the good things that have happened in the past 24 hours. Let the video of your day roll and then press pause so that you can thank God for those special moments.

2. Think about all the people who mean a lot to you and spend some time now thanking God for each of these precious people.

3. Think of the people that you find difficult to get on with and thank God for the way he is using these people to develop your spiritual muscles. Ask God for his special blessing on each of these people in your life.

4. Thank God for the gift of life itself, for health and for the privilege of knowing him. Try to imagine what your life would have been like without God.

5. Now just spend a few minutes allowing your feelings and prayers of gratitude to well up in your heart. Express these vocally or silently.

You've Got Mail – from Jesus!

Imagine Jesus sending you the following questions by email. What would you reply to each of his questions?

- What do you want me to do for you?
- Do you believe I can do this?
- Do you love me?

- Do you love me?
- Do you love me?

Finally, don't forget to give yourself a computer break. Have an email-free day or a computer-free week, so that you can really spend quality time with Jesus.

Emails I Wish I Hadn't Sent

Spend some time thinking about emails or letters that you wish you hadn't sent.

- Why are you unhappy that you sent them?
- What would you change if you could re-send them?
- Do you need to ask God for his forgiveness?

Now visualise the 'sent' box of your computer clearing and a blank screen appearing in front of you. Is there anything you can do to bless the people that you sent these emails to? Now ask God to be your Son-screen to help you filter out unhelpful emails before you send them.

Emails I Wish I Hadn't Received

Spend some time now thinking about emails or letters that you have received that have hurt you in some way. Some people have even been sacked by email. Allow the thoughts, words and actions to fill your mind again as you visualise Jesus alongside you.

- Is Jesus saying anything to you about these emails?
- With God's help, can you forgive the people who sent them?

Now visualise your 'in' box being emptied, with a message from God saying 'For I know the plans I have for you ... to prosper you not to harm you, plans to give you hope and a future' (Jeremiah 29:11).

Video Playback Your Day (Five Minutes)

> I will bless the Lord who guides me; even at night my
> heart instructs me (Psalm 16:7 NLT).

A mini review of the day is like a video playback. You relive moments on the video screen of your mind, by pressing the *replay* button, and then you use the *pause* button to re-live or savour particular moments.

- Allow yourself to review the key moments of today.
- Replay and pause (freeze) those moments that you were happiest with ...
- Now thank God for those special times.
- Replay and pause (freeze) those moments that you were unhappy with ...
- Ask God to help you to deal better with these thoughts and situations in the future, and where necessary ask for his forgiveness.

In the same way, you could also video playback your week.

Going Deeper Into God (Five Minutes)

This meditation is adapted from my CD *A Quiet Place*.

1. Sitting or lying in a comfortable position with your eyes closed, spend some time focusing on your breathing, allowing it to become deeper and slower.

2. Relax your whole body and feel the tension melting away as you continue to breathe in deeply and out slowly.

3. Our relationship with God began in a garden. Imagine yourself in a beautiful garden now. Visualise its beauty – the colours, the aromas, the sounds. This is a special place for you to spend time with God, a place where he is drawing you to himself. It is a place of intimacy where you can share your heart's desires or simply enjoy his company.

4. Now accept Jesus' invitation to meet with you there . . . 'My lover spoke and said to me, "Arise, my darling, my beautiful one, and come with me"' (Song of Songs 2:10). You might want to play some music at this point.

Experiencing the Healing Power of God's Love (Fifteen-Minute Meditation)

This meditation draws upon my own experience of healing from ME and is taken from my CD *A Quiet Place*[13]. You might find it helpful to play some relaxing instrumental music during this meditation.

Script

Lie down in a warm, comfortable room where you won't be disturbed. You may want to have a small pillow behind your head and another pillow supporting any part of your body that's particularly painful. Alternatively, you may want to lie on a bed or the sofa.

I want you to imagine that your body has become a glass vessel and that there are small plugs at the end of each finger and toe. Inside this vessel is a grey murky liquid. Perhaps this grey liquid represents illness, pain, anger, bitterness or unforgiveness. Allow God to take this murky liquid from you now as he gently removes the imaginary plugs from your hands and feet.

Feel the liquid as it begins to drain from your head ... and skull ... down your neck ... and shoulders ... and along each arm. Feel it now as it drains through your elbows ... your wrists ... and hands ... and then out through the end of each finger. The grey murky liquid then continues to flow down your body ... through your torso ... along your spine ... down into your hips ... and thighs ... along your legs ... behind your knees ... into your ankles ... and out through the ends of each toe.

Now imagine that God is putting the plugs back in the end of each finger and toe ... and that Jesus is standing behind you with a large jug full of the most beautiful golden liquid – an expression of his love for you, for he longs to bring healing and restoration to your whole body.

Imagine Jesus pouring this beautiful warm golden liquid into you now. Feel it gently circulating around the inside of your head filling all the empty spaces ... and then flowing gently down your neck into your shoulders ... Feel its warmth and radiance as it flows along your arms . . . and out to each finger. Feel this wonderful glow beginning to fill your whole body, as it cleanses, repairs and heals. Feel the warmth as it continues to flow down your back . . . gently flowing into your hips . . . and thighs. Feel the warmth circulating around your knees . . . and ankles . . . right to the ends of each toe . . . your whole body bathed in light . . . Imagine your immune system building up as you feel God's presence re-energising you – and breathing new life into you.

Now allow God to continue enfolding you in his love. You might want to play a beautiful worship song focusing on God's love to finish.

DIY Relaxation and Meditations

Once you've got the hang of meditating, you might like to have a go at preparing your own meditations based on some of the ideas in this book. You could use Scripture from any part of the Bible and adapt some of the techniques I've used. I find there is a real wealth of material in Isaiah, Psalms, Proverbs and just about any part of the New Testament. You can even explore a particular theme. The Internet or a Bible CD-ROM will help you to compare different translations of the same text at the same time. You can always save them and print them out later to meditate on. You can even meditate interactively on the Internet. There are many sites that you could visit including Sacred Spaces which is run by the Jesuits. Their website guides you through ten minutes of prayer and meditation. On another website you can even walk around a virtual labyrinth which is an ancient Christian way of praying and meditating.

∞ Leading a Relaxation and Meditation Session for the First Time

Leading a relaxation and meditation session requires preparation, prayer and practice. Unfortunately, it is only as you begin to lead sessions that you learn what to do and you often learn most from your mistakes. Initially, as a leader, you will not be able to join in the session yourself because you will need to be aware of everyone in the room and be sensitive to the Holy Spirit. A friend of mine led a workshop for her church for the first time recently, so I asked her to write up what she learned from the experience.

> Several weeks ago I was asked to lead a half-hour workshop for our church's annual weekend away. I've never done this before and a feeling of panic flashed through me! I had been listening to your CD *A Quiet Place* and also reading your book *Out of the Depths* recently, and it suddenly occurred to me that I had enough material to put a relaxation session together.
>
> We had agreed that I would lead the next part of the session with an adaptation of your relaxation/meditation exercise where the listener imagines that he/she is a glass vessel full of grey murky liquid. There were probably about thirty adults in a large sitting-room for this. I asked the younger members of the group if they would like to lie on the carpet, so that the older members could have the sofas and armchairs. The room was transformed with bodies crashed out everywhere. While I was reading through the script, I was thinking about certain individuals in the room who had been

through very difficult times, and I asked God to really use this session to bring his healing and peace into their lives.

Most people looked very relaxed, eyes closed, stretched out and peaceful. Two people fell asleep and one of these started snoring! One person began sneezing because of dust on the carpet, and one person next to the door ended up as a bouncer, to stop the unwelcome interruptions from children. However, many people came up to me afterwards and thanked me for a wonderful session and said how much they enjoyed it. On reflection, I think there were a few things that I should have done differently:

1. Posted someone on the door beforehand to stop interruptions.

2. Spoken to the lady who was upset and told her that it was fine for her not to join in if she preferred.

3. Check that no one who had a dust allergy was going to lie on the floor.

4. I'm not sure about the snoring; perhaps I should have said that people could nudge the person next to them if their snoring got too loud!

5. I should have rounded the session off better with a prayer for everyone and pointed people towards appropriate books, music and relaxation and meditation CDs, and so on.

6. It would have been helpful for everyone to have taken away a verse of Scripture with them like 'Come with me by yourselves to a quiet place and get some rest' (Mark 6:31), to remind everyone of the importance of taking 'time out' for rest and refreshment.

∽ How Does a Meditation or Contemplative Prayer Group Work?

There are many established contemplative prayer and meditation groups across the world. You could find out about local Christian groups either by searching the Internet or by contacting your nearest convent, monastery, retreat centre or your local church. If there isn't a local group, you could always consider starting one yourself. Some groups don't have a specific leader, but each member takes it in turns to lead. The contemplative prayer group that I've been a part of for the past thirteen years meets once a month and is organised as follows:

The morning begins at 10.00 a.m., and we can arrive between 10.00 and 10.30 a.m. We chat in the kitchen over coffee and biscuits. This enables everyone to touch base with each other and creates a sense of community and sharing. It also gives people time to arrive so that we can start promptly at 10.30 a.m. without disrupting the session. The transition into quiet is made easier because we know that when we enter the lounge this is our sacred space for the session, and we endeavour not to bring our coffee, conversation or any other business in with us. Confidentiality is something that has already been established within our group so we know that it is safe to share revelations, thoughts and feelings at the end of the session.

10.00–10.30 a.m. We meet in the kitchen for refreshments.

10.30 a.m. We move into the lounge together. The leader introduces the theme and outlines the structure of the session.

10.45–11.00 a.m. The leader begins with a stillness exercise which may include a breathing exercise and possibly some music.

11:00 a.m. A Bible passage is read (it often relates to a particular theme) and time is given to reflect on this passage silently as a group. Questions might be asked to stimulate reflection. There may also be an opportunity to explore visual material.

11.15–11.45 a.m. Half an hour is then spent individually in silence, reflecting on the passage of Scripture and listening to God. Some people scribble in their journals, while others explore any visual material. I usually find it helpful to go into the garden.

The leader then draws us all back together and closes this part of the session in prayer, thanking God for his presence with us. She also prays a short prayer for the other members of the group who were unable to join us on this occasion.

11.45 a.m.–12.15 p.m. We have a feedback session for those who want to share afterwards. If people need to leave early, they can do so during this time. I have sometimes found this part of the morning to be the most valuable part, especially if I've struggled to receive anything from the session myself. I'm often amazed at the insights gained by others and it really encourages my faith.

∾ Relaxation and Meditation as Outreach

As I've already mentioned, meditation can be a natural bridge to evangelism. Consequently, I'm often asked for relaxation and meditation material that can be used in a secular context. Much of the material in this book could be used with non-Christians if it were adapted appropriately. It is also quite possible to lead non-Christians in Christian meditation providing you have informed them in advance. Here are some meditations, though, which you could use in a secular context.

The Beach Meditation (Five Minutes)

This meditation is one I devised for the Christian spirituality outreach course *Essence*[14] which is an excellent tool for evangelism. You will find it helpful to play some gentle atmospheric music during this meditation.

Script

Imagine that you are lying on a beach . . . think about your favourite beach and visualise yourself lying there now.

The pebbles are moving gently as the waves lap on to the shore . . . See the colours all around you – reflected in the sea . . . the shells . . . the sky . . .

Feel the warmth of the sun on your body as you relax into the warm sand beneath you. *(pause)*

Now imagine that you have become one of the pebbles on the beach . . .

How does it feel to be gently lifted up as the waves lap over you – refining . . . smoothing . . . redefining. *(pause)*

Enjoy the rhythm of the sea washing over you as you breathe out tension . . . and breathe in tranquillity; *(pause)* and as you breathe out anxiety . . . and breathe in peace. *(pause)*

Now think of those times when the tide of your life's circumstances have smoothed away your own rough edges.

(pause) And now thank God for his healing work in your life. *(pause)*

And finally, entrust yourself into the loving arms of the One who gives us the gift of his rest. *(let music play out)*

TV Meditation (Ninety Seconds)

This is the script of a meditation I led on mainstream TV recently. It was filmed on location at a local beauty spot.

Script

Let's focus on our breathing. Become aware of your breathing deepening and slowing . . .

Now visualise a beautiful lake . . . and imagine any stress and tension dropping to the bottom of the water like stones.

See the sun as it breaks through the clouds . . . feel its warmth . . . bathe in its light.

Savour the tranquillity of this scene as you continue to breathe in peace, and breathe out anxiety.

Become aware of the birdsong around you . . . and observe the swans as they glide majestically along the water's surface.

Now imagine yourself soaring free like a bird . . . leaving all your worries behind you.

> For those who hope in God
> will renew their strength
> They will soar on wings like eagles;
> they will run and not grow weary,
> they will walk and not feel faint.
>
> (My adaptation of Isaiah 40:31)

Book Shop Relaxation! (Five Minutes)

Yes, believe it or not I led this relaxation on the fifth floor of a busy book shop during Mental Health Week. I even had a broadcaster from the BBC join in too.

Script

I want you to make yourself comfortable either sitting or lying down, while I lead you in a gentle relaxation.

Now as you relax, just close your eyes . . . and become aware of your breath as it enters and leaves your body.

Notice the movement of your rib cage as you breathe . . .

Now notice the position of your arms and hands . . . and the position of your feet and legs.

Notice the feel of your clothing on the chair or floor beneath you.

Become aware of how your body is feeling. Are there any aches or pains? Do you feel alert and energised, or tired and lethargic? . . .

Now extend your awareness to the room around you . . . the floor . . . the walls . . . the ceiling and now extend that awareness to the world beyond this building . . .

Listen to the sounds that you can hear – traffic, people talking . . .

Extend your awareness as far as you can so that you become an observer of this world that you are a part of . . .

Now bring your attention back to this room . . . to your breath as it enters and leaves your body . . . and become aware again of yourself sitting or lying in this room feeling the breath enter and leave.

Continue to breathe in deeply and out slowly . . .

Enjoy the peace and stillness of the moment, thanking God for such a precious gift.

Gradually open your eyes and begin to familiarise yourself with your surroundings again. Have a good stretch and don't forget to smile!

Workplace Meditation (Five Minutes)

Think about the place where you work and form a picture of it in your mind ...

Now imagine yourself in this workplace ... Become aware of how you feel when you are there ...

Bring to mind all the positive things about your workplace and savour these positive aspects of your job in your imagination ...

Now bring to mind all the negative things about your workplace and enter into these in your imagination ...

Imagine these positive and negative responses to your workplace as being two separate rooms. In your imagination, see yourself walking backwards and forwards between the two rooms taking the more positive feelings and experiences with you into the negative environment ...

Now take your mind completely off work and have some fun. Replay and relive a practical joke, a funny situation or experience, a humorous scene from a film or video etc. Anything that makes you smile or laugh.

Is there any way you can take some of this sense of fun with you into the rest of your life?

Quick Relaxation (Five Minutes)

This short relaxation will help to calm your mind and relieve stress and tension.

Sit comfortably with your head supported. Close your eyes and focus on your breathing. Breathe in deeply and out slowly several times.

Now imagine that you are in one of your favourite places. It could be a beach, a countryside scene, a beautiful building . . . Savour the colours . . . the sounds . . . and the aromas around you . . . Relax and enjoy this calming environment.

Stay with this scene for as long as you can, so that your body and mind begin to feel calm and refreshed.

When you are ready, open your eyes gradually and become aware of your surroundings again.

CHAPTER 5

Keeping Spiritually Fit

~~✺~~

'EVERYTHING COMES TO THOSE WHO CAN'T WAIT!'

This advertising slogan for a loan company neatly sums up our fast-food, fast-living, credit-card, buy-now-pay-later culture. We've lost the ability to wait. For anything! Many of us spend tomorrow's prosperity today, because we've been sold the fantasy that we can have it *all,* and have it *now.* Patience is an old-fashioned word from the past; everything now is '2go', and even the lunch break is a thing of the past. We live life at such a frantic pace, is it any wonder that serious health problems are on the increase?

So where does God fit in?

God frequently requires us to wait patiently. His timing, though, is always perfect. My own impatience means that I frequently operate in my own strength and in so doing, I wear myself out. But this is not God's way. Anything he calls us to do, we can do with what the *Amplified Bible* describes as 'holy ease'.

Shortly before I was ill with burnout, a friend had a mental image of me running down the road distributing books with God running behind, trying to catch up with me!

Another friend had envisioned me dancing, and somehow I was no longer in control but was being danced at a frantic pace. This reminded me of the classic Hollywood film *The Red Shoes*, in which the ballet shoes dance the dancer into a frenzy.

During this precious recovery period, however, *the* most wonderfully romantic images of God dancing with me appeared on the video screen of my mind! As God twirled me round the dance floor like Fred Astaire and Ginger Rogers, I simply responded to his leading.

Dancing with God is an expression of great intimacy and love and one that means a great deal to me, because of my passion for dance. I am learning that the closer I am to God, the more likely I am to dance to his tune and at his speed.

Ask Yourself

- Do you ever run ahead of God?
- Which areas in your life are out of balance?

Take a few moments now to reflect on Isaiah 40 making it your own personal prayer. You might want to incorporate your name into Scripture, such as: 'But . . . Liz, if you trust in me, you will find new strength. In fact, you will rise up and soar like an eagle. You will walk and run without getting worn out,' referring to Isaiah:

But those who wait for the Lord [who expect, look for, and hope in Him] shall change and renew their strength and power; they shall lift their wings and mount up [close to God] as eagles [mount up to the sun]: they shall run and not be weary, they shall walk and not faint or become tired. (Isaiah 40:31 AMP)

∞ God Takes a Break and So Should We

> God saw all that he had made, and it was very good.
> (Genesis 1:31)

Can you remember when you last felt really satisfied with something you achieved and had the time to sit back and enjoy it?

Life is lived at such a frantic pace now that no sooner do we finish one task than we have to start the next. We may even be multitasking too. Sometimes I'm juggling the writing of several books at one go, which makes it difficult to appreciate anything I create. This is not how I want to live my life, but it is not easy to put the brakes on unless you are forced to through illness.

I wonder if you feel overwhelmed at the moment? Genesis tells us that even God took a break and the first thing Adam and Eve did was to rest and enjoy God's presence. 'And on the seventh day God ended His work which He had done; and He rested on the seventh day from all His work which He had done' (Genesis 2:2 AMP).

∞ It's Not Only Your Mobile Phone That Needs Recharging!

> And God blessed (spoke good of) the seventh day,
> set it apart as His own, and hallowed it, because on it
> God rested from all His work which he had created
> and done. (Genesis 2:3 AMP)

Sabbath rest is not an option for Christians; it is a commandment: 'Six days you shall labour and do all your work. But the seventh day is a Sabbath to the LORD your God. On it you shall not do any work' (Exodus 20:9–10). Sunday is now a working day for many and so has become indistinguishable from the rest of the week. In our 24-7 culture, we no longer benefit from the special status of a day of rest, so it is hardly surprising that we are reaping the consequences.

Christians are called to live differently, to be 'in the world' but not 'of it'. It is hard, however, to resist being sucked into the success-driven, work-orientated, time-crunching nature of our culture, where taking regular breaks or even a day off has become a thing of the past. It's been said that those suffering with burnout are simply making up for all the Sabbaths they haven't taken off to rest.

Ask Yourself

What are the different ways you enjoy resting and relaxing? You might want to list these to remind you to make them a priority in your life. When your life gets too busy, these are the things that get squeezed out!

Workaholism seems to be applauded in our culture, and if people burn out as a result of overwork, they now seem to be as expendable as a printer cartridge. Two close friends of mine with top jobs have just had to resign through ill health as a result of stress and burnout. The relentless pressure of their jobs has caused them to become ill, and yet they have worked long and hard giving the best years of their lives to their companies. Now, because they cannot function at the same level of efficiency, they have been encouraged to leave. Effectively, at the ages of forty-five and fifty, they have both been traded in for newer and younger models.

Many people in ministry do not practice what they preach. I am a prime example. But, when we go against God's laws, there are always consequences. I've been paying the price of breaking those laws and have had to learn how to change my bad working habits and seek God's divine timetable. I have come to accept that workaholism is an addiction and an illness. Just like an addict, I have to fight off the compulsion to secretly squeeze in extra work. Ignoring the importance of the Sabbath rest has spiritual and physical consequences. I have had to repent of breaking one of God's fundamental laws. It's not easy to change ingrained habits, but with God's transforming power anything is possible.

Ask Yourself

- Do you take enough rest? Try asking your friends and family whether you do.
- Do you need to lay down your work schedule so that God can show you his divine timetable for your life?

- When you pray, try laying your diary open before God. What thoughts enter your mind? Make a note of anything you think God might be saying to you.

Therefore, since the promise of entering his rest still stands, let us be careful that none of you be found to have fallen short of it . . . Now we who have believed enter that rest.
(Hebrews 4:1, 3 TNIV)

∞ My Diary of Burnout

No man is worthy to succeed until he is willing to fail.
A. W. Tozer [15]

I remember reading an article by a friend and well-known Christian leader, exploring the idea of New Year resolutions. He had decided, despite his busy schedule, to make time for people in 2003. My rather superspiritual response to this was that I wanted to make more time for God. Anyway, friends had to be fitted in around my very important work for God!

For me, the first few months of 2003 were manic with even more pressure being put on me to write yet more books. This popularity fed my workaholism, my need to be needed and my anxiety as I feared losing contracts if I told various publishers to wait. So with work in the front seat and me driving at the wheel, God was forced into the back, or even the boot and I was heading for a crash. I had become driven by work rather than led by God. A punishing schedule of more books, radio and TV broadcasts and Christian conferences followed, and then six months into 2003, while I was writing this book, I crashed. Not a very good witness for someone who writes books on stress and leads Christian relaxation and meditation sessions! Even more embarrassingly my publication *The Thing about the Office*, which gives tips on dealing with workplace stress, was just about to be published. I felt like such a failure, unable to practise what I preach.

So where had I gone wrong? How and why had I allowed myself to become driven beyond the call of God? What was at the root of my drivenness?

I later discovered that the root cause was fear. Fear drives but the Lord leads, and fear is in direct opposition to faith. Then I came across this quote by Henri Nouwen, a well-known contemplative and spiritual leader:

> God does not want you to destroy yourself. Exhaustion, burnout, and depression are not signs that you are doing God's will. God is gentle and loving. God desires to give you a deep sense of safety in God's love. Once you have allowed yourself to experience that love fully, you will be better able to discern who you are being sent to in God's name.[16]

'Similarities between you and your computer – both crash when overloaded!'[17] This is the opening line from my book *The Thing about Stress*, and it proved to be something of a prophetic statement. My main computer crashes frequently – virtually every time I send an email – and my laptop won't even recharge because the battery has packed up.

What an accurate picture of burnout! I could no longer do anything, I couldn't think straight, make a decision, write, deal with my mail or email. I was all charged out, running on empty. Furthermore, it felt as though I was drowning in a sea of my own books. I was unable to write the new ones which were now in a delayed queuing system and unable to cope with or even enjoy the new publications as they arrived hot off the press at my front door.

In fact, the arrival of my own publications now made me feel sick because it represented yet more work in the form of promotion, marketing and connecting with publishers and the media. I was out of energy. No light appeared on my laptop as I tried to recharge it. It simply wouldn't work, and neither could I.

In addition, when I sat at my computer, pins and needles would shoot up my arms, and I'd get pain in my elbows making it impossible to do anything but open the odd email. Writing by hand was also painful, and so that was severely limited. Six months before I had pleaded with God to show me new ways of working and this is exactly what he was doing, so why was I surprised?

During this time, however, I learned how to let go of being Miss Multi-Capable-Independent-Person and learned how to rely totally on God and his provision through other people. It's been a very humbling experience, to be physically incapable of doing something as basic to my job as type or even click a mouse. I purchased a voice software package which was rather like trying to train a naughty puppy dog to hear and respond to my voice. What a wonderful illustration of my own endeavours to hear and obey God!

In many ways, even the problem with my arms have been a blessing because it has given me a chance to rest and recover from exhaustion. Had I been physically able at that time, I would have been tempted to cheat the recovery process and carry on writing. But RSI (repetitive strain injury) stopped me in my tracks so that I became totally dependent on God. I had surrendered control at last.

It took me six months to recover from burnout, during which time I lived with a friend so that I could escape the continuous demands made via voicemail, letter and email, and take quality time out. Most authors like to go away to write, I went away to get away from writing because I was all written out!

A workaholic is someone who is so addicted to work that they can't bear to do without it. That was me, and I simply didn't know how to change. I knew that only God could help me because my attitudes and habits were so ingrained– and that is what this precious time has been about. I was no longer in the fast lane, God rescued me from the motorway of life where I had broken down on the hard shoulder and took me off in his recovery vehicle to hospital. In a sense, God had rescued me from myself. He was answering my cry for help, 'Lord, help me to work differently. I can't go on like this.'

Another prayer I used to pray with great frustration was 'Lord, show me how to stop turning everything I receive from you into another book.' Any personal revelations I received from God, I saw as material for books. I had a problem with receiving because I was so focused on achieving.

I would like to think my main motive was so unselfish that I was simply wanting to give out to others, but in reality it was a sign that the 'achievement orientated junkie' I referred to when writing my book on ME, was still alive and kicking. Hadn't suffering with ME been a big enough lesson for me to learn from? God healed me of that illness thirteen years ago, and yet I'm still wrestling with the same drivenness that caused me to be ill in the first place.

∞ The Ultimate Makeover

Our TV in the UK is awash with lifestyle makeover programmes, some of which we've been kind enough to export to America! It's reached saturation point here, though the cash tills of the DIY shops are still ringing. But only God can give us a real makeover. He cares about every detail of our lives.

As I work from home, my home also needs to be my place of rest and leisure. While I was living away, I gained perspective not only spiritually, but practically too. I could see that my house needed a radical overhaul so that it could be set up for normal life again. I had allowed work to dominate my house with paperwork and books everywhere, even on the stairs. I just couldn't escape from work. No wonder I felt that I could no longer invite anyone round.

When I made a list of my main stressors, one of them was the state of decoration of my house, and another was my lack of organisation and filing systems. The answer to the first stressor was simple, get a decorator in. Another friend, gifted in administration and organisational systems offered to help me sort and file, while another friend cleared my overgrown garden and restored it to its original beauty. He also lovingly planted new seeds and bulbs. The house and garden became a picture of what God was doing in my life. He was clearing out the rubbish, cutting back the dead wood, healing past wounds and sowing for the future. I was like a bulb, drawing nourishment from him, while I remained hidden in order to replenish my reserves. I was in a special place of safety and protection held in his love and care. It was as though a sign had been erected saying, 'Do not disturb, God at work.'

What an investment of time this has been. I have learned the true meaning of being hidden in Christ and my prayer journal has never filled up so quickly! Living away from home with friends in community has been a very special experience and made me realise my desire for companionship. Work had always overruled this need before and anyway, a partner might get in the way of my very important work for God! I had allowed work to become an idol elevating it above every area of my private life. But now I was beginning to value relationships in a new way and see friends as a special gift from God.

As this book explores intimacy with God, it is hardly surprising that God rescheduled my schedule while I have been writing it. I may not have been able to write the book for six months, but I was living it, and this has inevitably led to me writing a very different book. Thank goodness God's agenda superseded mine. I was going to whip through certain sections of this book, especially the Bible meditations. What could I have been thinking of? I was not operating out of God's anointing but out of my own stress and pressure.

God is the ultimate time manager. His way might seem to take longer and on this occasion it stretched the deadline, but his timing is always perfect. The writing of this book highlights my own human weakness and frailty, but it magnifies God's strength and power to transform any situation. I really thank God that he uses cracked pots like me!

∞ I've Had Enough, Lord

In the desert of overwork and exhaustion everything looks bleak. Elijah was so depressed that he wanted to die! There have been many times when I have dreamt of running away somewhere just like David, 'Oh for wings like a dove, to fly away and rest! I would fly to the far off deserts and stay there. I would flee to some refuge from the storm' (Psalm 55:6–8 LB). Even Jesus, when he met the Samaritan woman, was not only thirsty but exhausted. 'Jesus, tired from the long walk, sat wearily beside the well' (John 4:6 NLT).

But, as we spend time in God's presence we can be refreshed and restored. Elijah was so overwhelmed by his circumstances that he took a physical, spiritual and emotional nose dive. This can happen so easily to us if we don't rest and spend enough time in God's presence. God met Elijah's needs by giving him what was effectively his own personal retreat! Have you said, 'I've had enough, Lord' recently? Are you desperate for time off and time out with God? How about considering a retreat. Think about the following options:

Going on Holiday with God!

So what is a retreat? A retreat is essentially a special holiday with God. People used to consider retreats as being just for very religious people, but nowadays even people on the edge of church life are taking retreats. Many people are losing sight of the meaning of life and are searching for something to fill that deep spiritual hunger within. So it is not surprising that retreats are becoming popular.

A retreat is a wonderful opportunity to get away from everything and to nourish the parts of us that have become neglected. A retreat is also a decision to deepen our most important relationship, to spend quality time with God, to communicate with him not just at head level, but from the heart. It is also a time of adventure and exploration, a time to learn new ways of praying and listening to God and to increase our awareness of his presence in our lives.

Often, retreat houses are set in beautiful grounds, which can naturally help people to relax and feel closer to God. Some people have found retreats to be like a honeymoon period with God, while others see it as essential maintenance.

It's been said that 'to retreat is to advance'. When you take time out from the motorway of life, it is an investment, because you regain perspective. A friend of mine wrote this shortly after her recent retreat.

> I went on a four-day silent retreat, which I can only describe as life changing. I'm discovering that every time I take the trouble to get away with God, no matter what state I may think I'm in, he meets with me and I stand amazed at his faithfulness. I came away from the retreat with the sense of having a deep, deep well of quietness inside me, and also the questions: What could God do if I went away with him more often? If I sat at his feet and just waited for him to speak? These are questions to ponder.

There are many different types of retreat; silent retreats, preached retreats, themed retreats, creative-arts retreats, retreats in daily life, Ignatian retreats and many more. Retreats can be held in hotels, diocesan conference centres, monasteries, convents, people's homes and gardens. They can last from a day to a week – or even several weeks.

I have led ME retreats which take into account the specific needs of people who suffer with this illness. My focus on these retreats, however, is not the illness, but on helping each sufferer draw closer to God. Prayer is very difficult when you are ill and sufferers often feel isolated. Many feel distant not only from other Christians, but from God too.

So a retreat becomes a special time of friendship and fellowship. Some people receive considerable healing on retreat physically, spiritually and emotionally. I was healed of ME during our church weekend away at a retreat centre, and other sufferers have been healed on ME retreats that I have led. One severe sufferer literally got out of her wheelchair and walked after she was prayed for!

Going on retreat is a little like booking your car in for an MOT and service. Just as a car engine needs re-tuning so do we. In fact, one retreat centre advertises its retreats as '12,000 mile service for those in ministry'. Here is a spiritual MOT for you to try.

Giving Yourself a Spiritual MOT

Check Points:

- **Steering** – Who is in control of your life, you or God? 'Whether you turn to the right or to the left, your ears will hear a voice behind you, saying, "This is the way; walk in it"' (Isaiah 30:21).

- **Lights** – Can you see where you're going? 'Where there is no vision, [no redemptive revelation of God] the people perish' (Proverbs 29:18 AMP).

- **Bodywork** – Are you looking after your body? 'You know that your body is a temple where the Holy Spirit lives . . . God paid a great price for you. So use your body to honour God' (1 Corinthians 6:19–20 CEV).

- **Breaks** – Do you know when to stop? 'Jesus said, "Come with me by yourselves to a quiet place and get some rest"' (Mark 6:31 NIV).

- **Fuel** – Where does your energy come from? 'I, the LORD, have put a curse on those who turn from me and trust in human strength. They will dry up like a bush in salty desert soil, where nothing can grow. But I will bless those who trust me. They will be like trees growing beside a stream – trees with roots that reach down to the water, and with leaves that are always green' (Jeremiah 17:5–8 CEV).

- **Tyres** – Have you got a grip on life, or are you losing it? 'Don't let the world around you squeeze you into its own mould, but let God remake you so that your whole attitude is changed' (Romans 12:2 Ph).

- **Engine** – Are you tuned into God or yourself and your own desires and needs? 'My sheep listen to my voice; I know them, and they follow me' (John 10:27).

Suggestions for Retuning Your Life:

- **Control** – Keep surrendering control to God. Remember God's in the driving seat, not you.

- **Stop** – Take stock of who you are and the priority God has in your life. You could:

  1. Book yourself a break or go on a retreat. Even racing cars need pit stops!

  2. Keep a journal, which can be your spiritual log book.

  3. Consider receiving spiritual direction to help fine-tune your relationship with God.

- **Beam** – Keep your lights switched on. The Word of God lights up your path and illuminates your journey. So keep reading, studying and absorbing Scripture.

- **Watch** – What you read as well as what you view on the Internet, TV, video and DVD. Remember your eyes are the mirror to your soul.

- **Zoom** – God's speed not yours!

  1. Pray and take time to discern what God is really calling you to do.

  2. Don't forget to relax and enjoy yourself.

  3. What would you like to spend time doing? How can you make this possible?

  4. What would you like to do less often in your life? Is there any way you can bring this about?

  5. What hobbies or interests would you like to develop?

- **Bodywork** – You only have one body – there isn't a spare on the shelf. So look after your body and keep fit and healthy. Stick to a balanced diet, exercise regularly and get plenty of sleep.

Creation

Many of the psalms in the Bible remind us that God speaks to us through two books, the Bible and through the wonders of creation. Sometimes creation can speak in ways nothing else can. I was so stressed out and tired on one particular retreat weekend that I struggled to get anything out of it. I couldn't relate to any of the material or relax enough to hear or even find God! I may have stopped physically, but I was still running on the inside and heading for a crash.

When I went for a walk along a country lane nearby, however, the beauty and silence of the countryside helped me to start shedding the baggage of work. In the middle of the road, I saw a squashed frog which had obviously been mown down by a busy commuter. This really spoke to me. Not only could I identify with the frog who seemed to have had all the life squeezed out of it, but also with the fast pace of life which can so recklessly leave casualties in its wake.

Later on that day, I was able to pray, 'Lord, help me to switch off from work and in to you. Re-energise me by your presence, help me to plug in and switch on to you and recharge me through the power of the Holy Spirit, amen.'

The story of the two disciples walking the Emmaus Road reminds us that Jesus walks alongside us all the time in every aspect of our life. Next time you go for a walk, imagine him walking next to you, and see if there is anything he wants to say to you. Alternatively, you could just chill out and enjoy his company!

Spiritual Direction

Spiritual direction, or spiritual guidance, is becoming increasingly popular in all branches of the church today as Christians in ministry and leadership search for deep renewal and fresh direction.

The purpose of spiritual direction is to help a person deepen their relationship with God and become more aware of the presence of God in their lives. A spiritual director is someone who walks alongside, affirming and assisting the person in their prayer life and helping them to hear God and follow his leading. It is not counselling or therapy, because the focus of the meeting is the person's relationship with God.

My spiritual director describes herself as 'a spiritual sounding board', but she also offers me spiritual accountability, which I feel is very important in the work that I do. I see her once every two or three months and continue to find her guidance invaluable. I've also trained as a spiritual director and use many of the skills I've acquired in my various publications and when leading retreats. My spiritual director is an Anglican nun with a wonderful sense of humour, but a spiritual director does not have to be part of a religious community; they could be a minister or layperson. It is important to find the right person for you, however, so a trial period is usually advisable.

The Christian tradition of spiritual direction dates back to AD 330. Saint Augustine himself advised that 'no one can walk without a guide'. There are many examples of different types of spiritual direction in the Bible. On the Emmaus Road, the risen Christ himself walked alongside the two disciples helping them to make sense of what had happened to them (Luke 24:13–35).

In Paul's letter to Timothy, we see Paul encouraging Timothy in his calling:

> To Timothy, my dear son: Grace, mercy and peace from God the Father and Christ Jesus our Lord . . . For this reason I remind you to fan into flame the gift of God, which is in you through the laying on of my hands. For God did not give us a spirit of timidity, but a spirit of power, of love and of self-discipline. (2 Timothy 1:2, 6, 7)

Keeping a Journal

A journal is a personal and private record of our relationship with God. Whereas an engagements diary helps a person organise their time, a journal runs alongside time and reviews it. You write a journal in the way you might talk to a close friend. You can express anger and disappointment, give thanks and praise, outline your hopes and dreams, ask questions, write letters, copy Scripture, write down 'words', thoughts, images or ideas.

My journal is a very precious dialogue with God charting my journey of intimacy with him. Sometimes I draw in my journal, stick in photos, cards, dried flowers, prayers and emails, anything that has touched me in a special way. These are signs of God's love in my life.

As I've had physical difficulties writing, I've also been cutting out sections of my Bible and sticking these in too. This has been a very exciting development to my journaling and has helped bring the Bible to life for me. It also means that I now have certain Scriptures at my finger tips.

The journals I have kept across the past twelve years have become a real treasure, reassuring me of God's presence with me every step of the way. They chart the highs, the lows, the desert times and the long periods of waiting when nothing seems to be happening. Writing things down helps to clarify my thinking and enables me to remember precious gems I might otherwise forget.

If you want to grow in your relationship with God, I'd recommend keeping a journal. You don't need to worry about writing things down daily, instead enjoy the freedom and creativity of communicating with God whenever and however you like. God created us to live in a dynamic relationship of communication with him, and writing a journal is another one of the ways we can do this.

Exploring Creativity

God is our Creator Father and so we are naturally creative because we're made in his image. Creativity is a powerful form of communication and can help us to draw closer to God. God values all that we are and everything we create, however simple. He invites us to come as little children and to play in his presence.

Having spent many years training as a dancer, I find that the way I can draw closest to God is through dance. Dancing is a part of my prayer time too. When I run out of words to express how I feel, I simply move freely in the Spirit, interceding and worshipping God. When I dance, I am praying and moving from my heart, rather than from my head. Even King David danced before the Lord.

Dance is also a very powerful form of warfare. During burnout I was too exhausted to even think about dancing. When I attended a burnout retreat, however, one of the team, who didn't know my background, had the following 'word' for me from the Lord: 'She needs to come before me and dance in triumph over what I have done in her life and what I'm going to do. This will release her further as the enemy flees at the praising of my name. She not only praises me in her heart when she dances, every step, position and movement represents praise. It is as if the whole choir were singing praises in the spirit when she dances.'

A couple of years ago, when I was helping to pilot a Christian spirituality course, I led a session using clay. We were meditating on the theme 'The Journey So Far' and exploring painful things that had happened in our lives. We were also thinking about the sufferings of Christ. Each person had a lump of clay and a nail. One man, a minister had carefully created a ring of clay and pierced it right through with the nail from one side to the other. I found this a very powerful image. He explained that the clay ring represented his wedding ring and the nail the pain of his divorce. This activity helped him to get in touch with his feelings again and surrender them to God. In an atmosphere of prayer and trust, we were all able to share different aspects of our walk with God and receive healing.

I later led a similar activity at a Christian dance and healing day. This time our bodies were like clay, and we expressed painful experience from the past in movement whilst holding a large nail. When each person was ready to let go of their pain, they moved towards the cross and nailed it there. A great deal of healing and release into freedom took place that day.

Creativity is woven into Scripture in a whole variety of different ways (I've put the 'creative' words in italics):

- My frame was not hidden from You when I was being formed in secret [and] intricately and curiously wrought [as if *embroidered* with various colours] in the depths of the earth [the region of darkness and mystery] (Psalm 139:15 AMP).

- Let them praise His name in chorus and choir and with the [single or group] *dance*; let them *sing* praises to Him with the tambourine and lyre! (Psalm 149:3 AMP).

- She makes for herself coverlets, cushions and rugs of *tapestry* (Proverbs 31:22 AMP).

- Is not this David, the king of the land? Did they not *sing* one to another of him in their *dances* (1 Samuel 21:11 AMP).

- *Sing to Him, sing praises to Him*; meditate on and talk of all His wondrous works and devoutly praise them! (1 Chronicles 16:9 AMP).

- Remember [earnestly], I beseech You, that You have *fashioned to me as clay* [out of the same earth material, exquisitely and elaborately]. And will You bring me into dust again? (Job 10:9 AMP).

- Yet, O Lord, You are our Father; we are the *clay*, and You our Potter, and we all are the work of Your hand (Isaiah 64:8 AMP).

Retreat on the Streets!

One of the most unusual retreats I have ever attended is a 'Retreat on the Streets'. It took place for a whole day in Nottingham, the city where I live. The idea behind the retreat was to challenge participants to reflect on social injustice, poverty and homelessness. We met in a city centre church one winter morning and handed over all our money, credit cards, mobile phones, reading materials, and so on. We were then sent off for the day with only £1 to spend on food and drinks.

As the day spanned several meal times, I soon became aware of the limitations of choice that were imposed on me through lack of money. Did I buy a hot drink to warm me up, or did I buy some chips to help satisfy my hunger? I couldn't afford both.

As I wandered the streets I sensed God's heart for people serving in shops and for those who could only look but couldn't afford to buy. I had time to notice people, to talk to them, to pray for them. I could identify with those begging for money for food too.

I soon found out that shopping is no fun once the possibility of purchasing something is removed. In fact, it becomes a depressing experience. Time drags in a city when you can't afford to buy anything. What do you do? Where do you go?

In the six hours I wandered the streets, however, I felt as though I had connected with God's heart for the city in a way I had never done before. The city is an arid desert for many, but I will never forget that special day. Jesus identified with those on the margins of society, and we are called to do the same.

CHAPTER 6

The Bible Workout – A Spiritual Health Programme

❧

Finally, here is my Bible Workout programme that brings together many of the themes in this book.

Physically we are said to be getting lazier, fatter and less active and this can have a detrimental effect on our spiritual life. The fitness industry, however, is booming, and having a personal trainer seems to be a lifestyle necessity both here in the UK and America. But the toughest thing about exercising is getting started, it requires discipline. To be spiritually fit takes discipline too, but we have our own free personal trainer – God. At certain times of year we naturally focus on our body shape and levels of fitness, but I wonder how many of us think about our spiritual health. On a scale of 1–10, how would you rate your current spiritual fitness?

Well, I really want to encourage you to 'go for it', to spend time improving your spiritual health and fitness – it could be the best investment you ever make!

Okay, so let's get started:

∞ Getting in Shape

> Train yourself towards godliness (piety), [keeping yourself
> spiritually fit].
>
> 1 Timothy 4:7 AMP

Try warming up with these motivational Scriptures:

One-Minute Warm-Ups

Read slowly and reflectively

> Do you not know that your body is the temple (the very
> sanctuary) of the Holy Spirit Who lives within you, Whom
> you have received [as a gift] from God? You are not your own.
> You were bought with a price [purchased with a preciousness
> and paid for, made His own]. So then, honour God and bring
> glory to Him in your body. (1 Corinthians 6:19–20 AMP)
>
> I press on toward the goal to win the [supreme and heav-
> enly] prize to which God in Christ Jesus is calling us upward.
> (Philippians 3:14 AMP)

Five-Minute Warm-Ups

Read each Scripture through slowly and reflectively. What
is this passage saying to you? Which words have become highlighted? Is God saying anything to you through this passage?

> Therefore then, since we are surrounded by so great a
> cloud of witnesses [who have borne testimony to the Truth],
> let us strip off and throw aside every encumbrance (unnec-
> essary weight) and that sin which so readily (deftly and clev-
> erly) clings to and entangles us, and let us run with patient
> endurance and steady and active persistence the appointed
> course of the race that is set before us. (Hebrews 12:1 AMP)

Do you not know that in a race all the runners run, but only one gets the prize? Everyone who competes in the games goes into strict training. They do it to gain a crown that will not last; but we do it to get a crown that will last forever. Therefore I do not run like a man running aimlessly; I do not fight like a man beating the air. No, I beat my body and make it my slave so that after I have preached to others, I myself will not be disqualified for the prize. (1 Corinthians 9:24–27)

Next time you play sport, visit the gym, or go walking or jogging, keep these Scriptures in mind. You could even record them on a mini disc or cassette recorder and then you can plug into Scripture instead of the usual TV and pop videos that run endlessly at most gyms.

∞ Lifestyle Workouts

The following sections are quick one-minute meditations for you to reflect on and carry with you into your day. Just choose one a day from any section and focus your attention on it when you can.

Faith Builders

Faith building Scriptures to help develop your spiritual muscles.

- And without faith it is impossible to please God, because anyone who comes to him must believe that he exists and that he rewards those who earnestly seek him. (Hebrews 11:6 TNIV)

- Jesus replied, 'What is humanly impossible is possible with God.' (Luke 18:27 TNIV)

- Truly I tell you, if you have faith as small as a mustard seed, you can say to this mountain, 'Move from here to there' and it will move. Nothing will be impossible for you. (Matthew 17:20 TNIV)

- Everything is possible for one who believes. (Mark 9:23 TNIV)

- Then he touched their eyes and said, 'According to your faith will it be done to you'; and their sight was restored. (Matthew 9:29–30)

- Be imitators of God, therefore, as dearly loved children and live a life of love, just as Christ loved us and gave himself up for us. (Ephesians 5:1–2)

- (God) is able to [carry out His purpose and] do superabundantly, far over and above all that we [dare] ask or think [infinitely beyond our highest prayers, desires, thoughts, hopes, or dreams]. (Ephesians 3:20 AMP)

- He sent forth his word and healed them. (Psalm 107:20)

- Consequently, faith comes from hearing the message, and the message is heard through the word about Christ. (Romans 10:17 TNIV)

- If I have the gift of prophecy and can fathom all mysteries and all knowledge, and if I have a faith that can move mountains, but do not have love, I am nothing. (1 Corinthians 13:2 TNIV)

- We live by faith, not by sight. (2 Corinthians 5:7 TNIV)

- The only thing that counts is faith expressing itself through love. (Galatians 5:6 TNIV)

- I tell you the truth, anyone who has faith in me will do what I have been doing. He will do even greater things than these, because I am going to the Father. And I will do whatever you ask in my name, so that the Son may bring glory to the Father. You may ask me for anything in my name, and I will do it. (John 14:12–14)

- Let us all come forward and draw near with true (honest and sincere) hearts in unqualified assurance and absolute conviction engendered by faith (by that leaning of the entire human personality on God in absolute trust and confidence in His power, wisdom, and goodness), having our hearts sprinkled and purified from a guilty (evil) conscience and our bodies cleansed with pure water. (Hebrews 10:22 AMP)

- For we have heard of your faith in Christ Jesus [the leaning of your entire human personality on Him in absolute trust and confidence in His power, wisdom, and goodness]... (Colossians 1:4 AMP)

- My flesh and my heart may fail, but God is the strength of my heart and my portion for ever. (Psalm 73:26)

- Faith by itself, if it is not accompanied by action, is dead. (James 2:17)

Office Workout

Scriptures to help you become a God-pleaser rather than a man-pleaser.

- Simply let your 'Yes' be 'Yes', and your 'No', 'No'; anything beyond this comes from the evil one. (Matthew 5:37)

- Now am I trying to win the favour of men, or of God? Do I seek to please men? If I was still seeking popularity with men, I should not be a bond servant of Christ (the Messiah). (Galatians 1:10 AMP)

- Never overestimate yourself or be wise in your own conceits. (Romans 12:16 AMP)

- Stay away from stupid senseless arguments. These only lead to trouble, and God's servants must not be trouble makers. They must be kind to everyone, and they must be good teachers and very patient. (2 Timothy 2:23–24 CEV)

- See to it that no-one takes you captive through hollow and deceptive philosophy, which depends on human tradition and the basic principles of this world rather than on Christ. (Colossians 2:8)

- Blessed are you when people insult you, persecute you and falsely say all kinds of evil against you because of me. Rejoice and be glad because great is your reward in heaven. (Matthew 5:11–12)

- Be humble when you correct people who oppose you. Perhaps God will lead them to turn to him and learn the truth. (2 Timothy 2:25 CEV)

- Jesus said, 'Treat others as you want them to treat you.' (Matthew 7:12 CEV)

- See to it that no-one misses the grace of God and that no bitter root grows up to cause trouble and defile many. (Hebrews 12:15)

- So don't worry about how to answer the charges against you, for I will give you the right words and such wisdom that none of your opponents will be able to reply! (Luke 21:14–15 NLT)

- God blesses those who work for peace. (Matthew 5:9 NLT)

- You want something but don't get it . . . You do not have, because you do not ask God. (James 4:2)

- You are only hurting yourself with your anger. (Job 18:4 GNB)

- God has done it all! He sent Christ to make peace between himself and us, and he has given us the work of making peace between himself and others. (2 Corinthians 5:18 CEV)

- A man's wisdom gives him patience; it is to his glory to overlook an offence. (Proverbs 19:11)

- Don't be selfish . . . be interested in others . . . and what they are doing. (Philippians 2:3–4 NLT)

- Figure out what will please Christ, and then do it. (Ephesians 5:10 MSG)

- Yet the Lord is faithful, and He will strengthen [you] and set you on a firm foundation and guard you from the evil [one]. (2 Thessalonians 3:3 AMP)

- For if you forgive men when they sin against you, your heavenly Father will also forgive you. But if you do not forgive men their sins, your Father will not forgive your sins. (Matthew 6:14–15)

- Let his words enrich your lives and make you wise. (Colossians 3:16 LB)

- I want you to trust me in your times of trouble, so that I can rescue you, and you can give me glory. (Psalm 50:15 LB)

- Whatever may be your task, work at it heartily (from the soul), as [something done] for the Lord and not for men. (Colossians 3:23 AMP)

Here are some workplace one liners:

- Don't let the world squeeze you into its mould – (Romans 12:2 Ph)

- Be transformed (changed) by the [entire] renewal of your mind … (Romans 12:2 AMP)

- In kindness he takes us firmly by the hand and leads us into a radical life-change. (Romans 2:4 MSG).

- And all of you serve each other with humble spirits, for God gives special blessings to those who are humble. (1 Peter 5:5 LB)

- Do not … be dismayed … I will help you. (Isaiah 41:10 AMP)

- The Lord … understands how weak we are … (Psalm 103:13–14 NLT)

- Now, a person who is put in charge as a manager must be faithful. (1 Corinthians 4:2 NLT)

- But if you refuse to forgive others, your Father will not forgive your sins. (Matthew 6:15 NLT)
- Let us strip off every weight that slows us down, especially the sin that so easily hinders our progress. (Hebrews 12:1 NLT)

Stress-Busting Workout

- He gives power to the faint and weary, and to him who has no might He increases strength [causing it to multiply and making it to abound]. (Isaiah 40:29 AMP)
- Do nothing out of selfish ambition or vain conceit, but in humility consider others better than yourselves. (Philippians 2:3)
- I have learned the secret of being content in any and every situation, whether well fed or hungry, whether living in plenty or in want. I can do everything through him who gives me strength. (Philippians 4:12–13)
- Don't worry about tomorrow. It will take care of itself. You have enough to worry about today. (Matthew 6:34 CEV)
- Blessed (happy, fortunate, to be envied) is the man whom You discipline and instruct, O Lord, and teach out of Your law. That You may give him power to keep himself calm in the days of adversity. (Psalm 94:12–13 AMP)

- Therefore we do not become discouraged (utterly spiritless, exhausted, and wearied out through fear). Though our outer man is [progressively] decaying and wasting away, yet our inner self is being [progressively] renewed day after day. (2 Corinthians 4:16 AMP)

- Above all things have intense and unfailing love for one another, for love covers a multitude of sins [forgives and disregards the offences of others]. (1 Peter 4:8 AMP)

- He who dwells in the secret place of the Most High shall remain stable and fixed under the shadow of the Almighty [Whose power no foe can withstand]. I will say of the Lord, He is my Refuge and my Fortress, my God; on Him I lean and rely, and in Him I [confidently] trust! (Psalm 91:1–2 AMP)

- But those who wait for the Lord [who expect, look for, and hope in him] shall change and renew their strength and power; they shall lift their wings and mount up [close to God] as eagles [mount up to the sun]; they shall run and not be weary, they shall walk and not faint or become tired. (Isaiah 40:31 AMP)

- Take My yoke upon you and learn from Me, for I am gentle [meek] and humble [lowly] in heart, and you will find rest [relief and ease and refreshment and recreation and blessed quiet] for your souls. (Matthew 11:29 AMP)

- Commit everything you do to the Lord. Trust him to help you do it and he will. (Psalm 375 LB)

- As pressure and stress bear down on me, I find joy in your commands. (Psalm 119:143 NLT)

- You will guard him and keep him in perfect and constant peace whose mind [both its inclination and its character] is stayed on You, because he commits himself to You, leans on You, and hopes confidently in You. (Isaiah 26:3 AMP)

- And the servant of the Lord must not strive . . . but be . . . patient. (2 Timothy 2:24 KJV)

- Let us strip off every weight that slows us down, especially the sin that so easily hinders our progress. (Hebrews 12:1 NLT)

- And all of you serve each other with humble spirits, for God gives special blessings to those who are humble. (1 Peter 5:5 LB)

- I refuse to be corrupt or to take part in anything crooked, and I won't be dishonest or deceitful. (Psalm 101:3–4 CEV)

- Base your happiness on your hope in Christ. When trials come, endure them patiently; steadfastly maintain the habit of prayer. (Romans 12:12 Ph)

Enemy Busters

Here are some Scriptures to help you stand firm when the enemy attacks.

- They overcame him by the blood of the Lamb and by the word of their testimony. (Revelation 12:11)

- And take the helmet of salvation and the sword that the Spirit wields, which is the Word of God. (Ephesians 6:17 AMP)

- The weapons we fight with are not the weapons of the world. On the contrary, they have divine power to demolish strongholds. (2 Corinthians 10:4)

- Jesus said to him, 'Away from me, Satan! For it is written: "Worship the Lord your God, and serve him only."' (Matthew 4:10)

- Jesus turned and said to Peter, 'Get behind me, Satan! You are a stumbling-block to me; you do not have in mind the things of God, but the things of men.' (Matthew 16:23)

- The God of peace will soon crush Satan under your feet. (Romans 16:20)

- Do not let the sun go down while you are still angry, and do not give the devil a foothold. (Ephesians 4:26–27)

- Submit yourselves, then, to God. Resist the devil, and he will flee from you. Come near to God and he will come near to you. (James 4:7–8)

- Finally, be strong in the Lord and in his mighty power. Put on the full armour of God so that you can take your stand against the devil's schemes. (Ephesians 6:10–11)

- The thief comes only in order to . . . kill and destroy. I came that they may have and enjoy life, and have it in abundance (to the full, till it overflows). (John 10:10 AMP)

- For God did not give us a spirit of timidity, but a spirit of power, of love and of self-discipline. (2 Timothy 1:7)

- The one who is in you is greater than the one who is in the world. (1 John 4:4)

- For I know the thoughts and plans that I have for you, says the Lord, thoughts and plans for welfare and peace and not for evil, to give you hope in your final outcome. (Jeremiah 29:11 AMP)

- The Lord will keep you from all evil; He will keep your life. (Psalm 121:7 AMP)

- And lead (bring) us not into temptation, but deliver us from the evil one. (Matthew 6:13 AMP)

- Do not be overcome by evil, but overcome evil with good. (Romans 12:21)

Sonbathing

Here are some great Scriptures to help you to relax and soak up the presence of God.

- Come with me by yourselves to a quiet place and get some rest. (Mark 6:31)

- Come to me, all you who are weary and burdened, and I will give you rest. (Matthew 11:28)

- The promise to enter the place of rest is still good, and we must take care that none of you miss out. (Hebrews 4:1 CEV)

- Yes, I will make springs in the desert, so that my chosen people can be refreshed. (Isaiah 43:20 NLT)

- Though her land is a desert, I will make it a garden. (Isaiah 51:3 GNB)

- When you pass through the waters, I will be with you; and when you pass through the rivers, they will not sweep over you. When you walk through the fire, you will not be burned; the flames will not set you ablaze. (Isaiah 43:2)

- Look to the LORD and his strength; seek his face always. (Psalm 105:4)

- You are my hiding place and my shield; I hope in your word. (Psalm 119:114 AMP)

- You are my hiding place; you will protect me from trouble and surround me with songs of deliverance. (Psalm 32:7)

- Keep me as the apple of your eye; hide me in the shadow of your wings. (Psalm 17:8)

- I will not forget you! See, I have engraved you on the palms of my hands. (Isaiah 49:15–16)

- For in the day of trouble He will hide me in His shelter; in the secret place of His tent will He hide me; He will set me high upon a rock. (Psalm 27:5 AMP)

- He has made my mouth like a sharp sword; in the shadow of His hand He hid me and made me a polished arrow in His quiver He has kept me close and concealed me. (Isaiah 49:2 AMP)

- Whoever has my commands and obeys them, he is the one who loves me. He who loves me will be loved by my Father, and I too will love him and show myself to him. (John 14:21)

- If you abide in My word [hold fast to My teachings and live in accordance with them], you are truly My disciples. (John 8:31 AMP)

- The words I have spoken to you are spirit and they are life. (John 6:63)

- Let the beloved of the LORD rest secure in him, for he shields him all day long, and the one the LORD loves rests between his shoulders. (Deuteronomy 33:12)

Soaking up the Psalms

Renew your strength and sharpen your focus as you allow these psalms to soak into your spirit.

Psalm 139:3 LB

You chart the path ahead of me, and tell me where to stop and rest.

Psalm 27:4 NLT

The one thing I ask of the Lord –
the thing I seek most –
is to live in the house of the Lord all the days of my life,
delighting in the Lord's perfections
and meditating in his Temple.

Psalm 42:1

As the deer pants for streams of water,
so my soul pants for you, O God.

Psalm 23:1–3 CEV

You, Lord are my shepherd,
I will never be in need.
You let me rest in fields of green grass.
You lead me to streams
of peaceful water,
and you refresh my life.

Psalm 131:2

But I have stilled and quieted my soul;
like a weaned child with its mother,
like a weaned child is my soul within me.

Psalm 121 NLT

I look up to the mountains –
does my help come from there?
My help comes from the LORD,
who made the heavens and the earth!
He will not let you stumble and fall;
the one who watches over you will not sleep.
Indeed, he who watches over Israel
never tires and never sleeps.
The LORD himself watches over you!
The LORD stands beside you as your protective shade.
The sun will not hurt you by day,
nor the moon at night.
The LORD keeps you from all evil
And preserves your life.
The LORD keeps watch over you as you come and go,
both now and forever.

Psalm 116:1–2 NLT

I love the Lord because he hears
and answers my prayers.
Because he bends down and listens,
I will pray as long as I have breath!

Psalm 145:14 NLT

The Lord helps the fallen
and lifts up those bent beneath their loads.

Psalm 107:15–16 NLT

Let them praise the LORD for his great love
and for all his wonderful deeds to them.
For he broke down their prison gates of bronze;
he cut apart their bars of iron.

Psalm 142:2 NLT

I pour out my complaints before him and tell him all
my troubles.

Psalm 119:93, 114, 162 NLT

I will never forget your commandments,
for you have used them to restore my joy and health.
You are my refuge and my shield;
your word is my only source of hope.
I rejoice in your word
like one who finds a great treasure.

Psalm 103:2–5 NLT

Praise the Lord, I tell myself;
and never forget the good things he does for me.
He forgives all my sins
and heals all my diseases.
He ransoms me from death
and surrounds me with love and tender mercies.
He fills my life with good things.
My youth is renewed like the eagle's!

Psalm 86:5, 10, 12–13 NLT

O Lord, you are so good, so ready to forgive,
so full of unfailing love for all who ask your aid.
For you are great and perform great miracles.
You alone are God.
With all my heart I will praise you, O Lord my God.
I will give glory to your name forever,
for your love for me is very great,
You have rescued me from the depths of death.

Psalm 16:7–8 NLT

> I will bless the Lord who guides me;
> even at night my heart instructs me.
> I know the Lord is always with me.
> I will not be shaken, for he is right beside me.

Psalm 139:17–18 LB

> How precious it is, Lord, to realise that you are thinking about me constantly! I can't even count how many times a day your thoughts turn towards me. And when I wake in the morning, you are still thinking of me!

∞ Spiritual Detox

> Let us all come forward and draw near with true (honest and sincere) hearts ... having our hearts sprinkled and purified from a guilty (evil) conscience and our bodies cleansed with pure water.
>
> Hebrews 10:22 AMP

I was praying with a friend recently when some really unpleasant images flooded my mind. I had been flicking through the TV channels to see if there was anything worth watching and, in doing so, saw images I would certainly not have chosen to see. With the sexualisation of almost everything on our TV screens, even flicking through various BBC TV channels is no longer a safe option. We absorb so much junk during the course of the day from TV, the Internet, through magazines, newspapers and billboards.

Our eyes are said to be the 'mirror of our souls' and our body is the temple of the Holy Spirit and so we need to be very selective about what we see and hear. 'The eye is the lamp of the body. So if your eye is sound, your entire body will be full of light. But if your eye is unsound, your whole body will be full of darkness' (Matthew 6:22–23 AMP).

Detox is a popular health and weight-loss regime, but I think we need a regular spiritual detox through the power of the Holy Spirit, to remove the build-up of polluting junk.

Try It Yourself

Ask God to show you if there are images and pictures lodged on the video screen of your mind. Now ask him to cleanse your mind and heart of these images. Visualise these images being washed away as though you were taking a shower, so that you are completely clean. Now picture something beautiful. It might be a favourite landscape or memory. Then meditate on this Scripture: 'Whatever is true, whatever is worthy of reverence and is honourable and seemly, whatever is just, whatever is pure, whatever is lovely and lovable, whatever is kind and winsome and gracious, if there is any virtue and excellence, if there is anything worthy of praise, think on and weigh and take account of these things [fix your minds on them]' (Philippians 4:8 AMP).

⮹ Spiritual Nutrition – The Good Food Guide for Strength and Growth.

So whether you eat or drink or whatever you do, do it all for the glory of God.

1 Corinthians 10:31 TNIV

The Good Food Guide

When we neglect the Word of God, we suffer from spiritual malnutrition. This becomes most evident during a crisis. The Word of God is our food; the Bible calls it our milk, bread, solid food and sweet dessert. It is not an optional extra for Christians, but a vital necessity.

Meditation has been described as 'chewing over' Scripture, and so it is a great way to digest and absorb food into our bodies so that it becomes spiritual fuel. Of course, we need regular doses of Scripture daily to stay strong and healthy.

Try savouring these Scriptures as you read through them slowly and reflectively. You might like to choose one from each section to meditate on, like a four course meal.

Milk

- Like newborn babies you should crave (thirst for, earnestly desire) the pure (unadulterated) spiritual milk, that by it you may be nurtured and grow unto [completed] salvation. (1 Peter 2:2 AMP)

- In fact, though by this time you ought to be teachers, you need someone to teach you the elementary truths of God's Word all over again. You need milk, not solid food! (Hebrews 5:12 TNIV)

Bread

- It is written: 'Man does not live by bread alone, but on every word that comes from the mouth of God.' (Matthew 4:4 NIV)

- I have treasured the words of his mouth more than my daily bread. (Job 23:12)

- Then the Lord said to Moses, 'I will rain down bread from heaven for you. The people are to go out each day and gather enough for that day. In this way I will test them and see whether they will follow my instructions.' (Exodus 16:4)

- Keep falsehood and lies far from me; give me neither poverty nor riches, but give me only my daily bread. (Proverbs 30:8)

- While they were eating, Jesus took bread, gave thanks and broke it and gave it to his disciples, saying, 'Take and eat; this is my body.' (Matthew 26:26 NIV)

- 'My food,' said Jesus, 'is to do the will of him who sent me and to finish his work.' (John 4:34 NIV)

Solid Food

- I gave you milk, not solid food, for you were not yet ready for it. Indeed, you are still not ready. (1 Corinthians 3:2)

- But solid food is for full-grown men, for those whose senses and mental faculties are trained by practice to discriminate and distinguish between what is morally good and noble and what is evil and contrary either to divine or human law. (Hebrews 5:14 AMP)

Sweet Dessert

- How sweet are Your words to my taste, sweeter than honey to my mouth! (Psalm 119:103 AMP)

- Eat honey, my son, for it is good; honey from the comb is sweet to your taste. Know also that wisdom is sweet to your soul; if you find it, there is a future hope for you, and your hope will not be cut off. (Proverbs 24:13–14)

∞ Finishing Strong

The Message translation of the Bible gives us some wonderful advice to encourage us to keep going

> Strip down, start running – and never quit! No extra spiritual fat, no parasitic sins. Keep your eyes on *Jesus*, who both began and finished this race we're in. Study how he did it . . . When you find yourselves flagging in your faith, go over that story again, item by item . . . *That* will shoot adrenaline into your souls! (Hebrews 12:1–3)

And just in case you were unable to unscramble the words and sentences on page 17 under the heading 'Information Overload', this forms the conclusion to my book!

> Hi there. Thanks for reading my book. It's great to share with you my passion for this very powerful form of prayer. My own journey into Christian meditation has been a life-changing adventure where I have learned how to draw close to the heart of God and to discern his leading for my life. This book comes from that place of seeking the Father's pres-

ence and listening to his voice and allowing him to direct my path. I pray that you are really blessed as you begin or continue your adventure into prayer. By the way, did you know that meditation was a natural stress buster and antidepressant? Some research studies show that it can even help you to live longer. Meditation is also a natural antidote to information overload. So do yourself a favour and take some time out with God. It could be the best investment you ever make!

I'd love to hear from you and to receive your feedback and ideas. You can contact me via my webpage,

www.lizbabbs.com or email, *liz@lizbabbs.com.*

Notes

1. Rev. Leonard C. Wilson, *Meditation – Why and How?* Pamphlet published by the Divine Healing Mission, East Sussex.
2. *Learning the Language of Prayer* © Joyce Huggett.
3. John Stott, quoted in *OC Team Newsletter* (spring 2002).
4. Henri Nouwen, *The Inner Voice of Love*, published and copyright 1997 by Darton Longman and Todd Ltd, and used by permission of the publishers.
5. 'Computer Psalm 23' – © 1998–2004, International Cyber Business Services, Inc.
6. Charles de Foucauld, quoted in Carlo Correto, *Summoned by Love* (London: Darton, Longman and Todd, 1978).
7. Adapted from 'Father's Love Letter' © 1999 Father Heart Communications.
8. Liz Babbs, *The Celtic Heart* (Oxford: Lion, 2003), 38.
9. Adapted from UCB's *Word for Today* by Bob Gass.
10. Brother Lawrence, *The Practice of the Presence of God* (London and Oxford: A. W. Mowbrays), 23.
11. Liz Babbs, *The Celtic Heart*, 32.
12. A meditation derived from Richard J. Foster's *Celebration of Discipline* (London: Hodder & Stoughton, 1989), 157.
13. Liz Babbs, *A Quiet Place* CD (Suffolk: Kevin Mayhew, 2004).
14. Rob Frost, *Essence* (Eastbourne: Kingsway Communications), 25.
15. A. W. Tozer, *Keys to a Deeper life*, copyright © 1957 by *Sunday Magazine*, 1987 by Zondervan. Used by permission of Zondervan.
16. Henri Nouwen, *The Inner Voice of Love*, 87–88.
17. Liz Babbs, *The Thing about Stress* (Oxford: Lion, 2002).

Permissions

In chapter 3, the text of the 'Father's Love Letter' was used by permission Father Heart Communications. Copyright 1999–2004, *www.FathersLoveLetter.com*.

Unless otherwise stated Scripture quotations are taken from *The Holy Bible, New International Version*, Copyright © 1973, 1978, 1984, by International Bible Society. Used by permission of Zondervan. All rights reserved.

Scripture quotations marked (TNIV) are taken from *The Holy Bible, Today's New International Version*™. Copyright © 2001 by International Bible Society. Used by permission of Zondervan. All rights reserved.

Scripture quotations marked (NLT) are from *The Holy Bible, New Living Translation*, copyright © 1996. Used by permission of Tyndale House Publishers, Inc.,Wheaton, Illinois 60189. All rights reserved.

Scripture quotations marked (LB) are from *The Living Bible*, copyright © 1971 Tyndale House Publishers, Inc., Wheaton, Illinois 60189. All rights reserved.

Scripture quotations marked (AMP) are from *The Amplified Bible*, copyright © 1954, 1958, 1962, 1965, 1987 by the Lockman Foundation. Used by permission.

Scripture quotations marked (CEV) are taken from *The Contemporary English Version Bible* © 2000 HarperCollins.

Scripture quotations marked (GNB) are taken from *The Good News Bible*, © 1966, 1971, 1976 American Bible Society.

Liz Babbs is a popular media interviewee who works extensively in the area of relaxations and meditation. Her work has been featured in many of the major newspapers and magazines, and she's recorded a series of stress-busting relaxation and meditation slots for Christian radio and TV. Her books include *The Thing about Stress*, *The Thing about the Office*, *The Thing about Calories*, *Out of the Depths*, *Can God Help M.E?* and *The Celtic Heart*. *A Quiet Place* is a CD of guided prayer, music and meditation.